ALTIUS FREEWING

Altius Freewing Books

A Philosophical Journey to Money, Control, and the Self

Unwritten: Write Your Fate

BHARANI VIR BHATLA

To the experiences that gave these pages life.

Most lives are scripted by circumstance; this book is for the few who dare to rewrite them.

Preface

Money is one of the most talked-about yet least understood subjects in our lives. Everyone has an opinion on how to earn, save, and invest, but if you take a step back, you'll realize that financial wisdom isn't a set of absolute truths—it's a collection of perspectives. As Nietzsche famously said, "There are no facts, only interpretations." This book is my interpretation of money, wealth, and the journey of financial independence. It's not a rulebook, nor is it a one-size-fits-all guide. It's simply my personal financial journey—full of wins, losses, lessons, and everything in between.

***

I didn't start out knowing everything about money. In fact, I made plenty of mistakes—some minor, some outright painful. I've invested in things I didn't fully understand, taken risks that didn't pay off, and ignored opportunities that, in hindsight, could have changed my life sooner. But that's how learning works. Trial and error, adjusting and improving along the way.

This book is for those who think like me—people who don't want financial jargon shoved down their throats but want to understand money in a way that actually makes sense. If you've ever felt lost in the sea of financial advice, unsure which strategy to follow, or frustrated by setbacks, you're not alone. My experiences won't give you an exact blueprint, but they might help you see things from a fresh perspective and build confidence in your own financial choices.

***

Most finance books are filled with strict rules, formulas, and "proven" strategies that promise to make you rich. But let's be real—money doesn't work that way. Context, mindset, and personal circumstances all play a massive role. This book doesn't claim to have the "right" way to manage money. Instead, it shares what worked for me, what didn't, and why.

Throughout the chapters, you'll learn not just what to do, but also what *not* to do. My goal isn't to hand you a checklist—it's to share my thought process, so you can think critically, apply what fits your life, and ignore what doesn't. Consider this book less of a map and more of a compass, helping you find your own way rather than forcing you down a set path.

These are lessons, and not Laws. Each chapter in this book is a lesson I learned firsthand. Some are about earning money, others about losing it. Some focus on the psychology of wealth, while others are straight-up practical. But every single one comes from real experience, not theories or secondhand advice.

***

Money is often misunderstood. Some people obsess over it, believing it's the key to happiness. Others dismiss it, acting like it doesn't matter. The truth, as I've learned, is somewhere in between. Money is a tool—a powerful one—that, when handled well, can give you freedom, security, and choices.

One thing I promise: no sugarcoating. I won't exaggerate my wins or downplay my losses. I won't act like I have all the answers, and I definitely won't make any ridiculous promises about getting rich overnight. What I *will* do is share my experiences exactly as they happened—the good, the bad, and the ugly.

If you've ever felt like traditional finance advice doesn't quite click with you, maybe my take will. My hope is that this book helps you find clarity, avoid some of the mistakes I made, and feel a little more in control of your financial future.

So, settle in, take what resonates, and let's get started.

***

Timeline of my journey

Every journey needs a map. Looking back, my financial path wasn't a straight road—it was a winding journey filled with risks, lessons, and unexpected detours. To fully grasp the insights in this book, it helps to see the key moments that shaped my financial mindset.

This isn't just a list of dates; it's a framework of pivotal experiences. Each moment influenced my decisions, refined my perspective on money, and contributed to my overall financial philosophy. By following this timeline, you'll see the challenges I faced, the calculated risks I took, and the milestones that defined my journey. My hope is that, in tracing my steps, you'll find insights that resonate with your own financial path.

***

Timeline of Key Moments

2006 – Graduated with a degree in Engineering, stepping into the real world with big dreams and little financial knowledge.

January 2007 – Started my first job at a bank—my introduction to the corporate world and financial systems.

April 2007 – Resigned from the bank, realizing early on that job satisfaction matters as much as a paycheck.

July 2007 – Joined a startup, embracing uncertainty, learning to take calculated risks, and understanding the value of adaptability.

May 2010 – Transitioned to my first Indian multinational corporation (MNC), stepping into a structured career path with better financial stability.

May 2011 – Took a leap into an international MNC, broadening my financial outlook and exposure to global markets.

July 2011 – Bought my first bike—a purchase driven by practicality and long-term value. A decision I stand by to this day.

January 2015 – Moved to the United States—a turning point that reshaped my approach to money, savings, and financial independence.

September 2015 – Bought my first car, a used one—balancing affordability with practicality, reinforcing the lesson that financial decisions should align with needs, not just desires.

January 2021 – Returned to India, bringing back a wealth of lessons from my international experience.

April 2021 – Groundbreaking ceremony for our new house—a milestone that symbolized years of disciplined financial planning.

December 2021 – Joined another Indian MNC, embracing new challenges while strategically positioning myself for growth.

> Relocated to a new city, adapting to a fresh financial landscape and recalibrating my financial plans.

February 2022 – Registered our new house, turning a long-term financial goal into a tangible reality.

October 2024 – Finally moved into our new home—proof that patience, discipline, and sound financial decisions pay off in the long run.

***

This timeline isn't just a sequence of events—it's a testament to financial growth, decision-making, and adaptability. Every choice I made—from switching jobs to buying my first bike—taught me something about money, risk, and long-term planning.

Throughout this book, you'll see how these moments shaped my financial philosophy. Each chapter follows a logical flow, distilling real-life lessons—some insightful, some tough, but all valuable. My hope is that by sharing my journey, you'll feel more confident in shaping your own.

***

Chapter 1: The Action Gap

We've all been there—sitting in a room, nodding along to a speaker, watching a financial guru on YouTube, or having a conversation with a friend. The advice is sound, the logic impeccable, and we find ourselves agreeing wholeheartedly. "Yes," we think, "I should definitely be doing that." But then... nothing. Days, weeks, months pass, and life continues as before.

This is the insidious Action Gap—the chasm between knowing and doing. And it's costing us dearly. Why do we fail to act? Let's cut to the chase: we're not ignorant. In fact, we are often well-informed, even experts in our own right. So why the disconnect? Why do we consistently fail to bridge the gap between knowledge and action?

Think about it. You know you should save a portion of your income. You know you should invest for the long term. You know you should avoid high-interest debt. Yet, the credit card bill arrives, the impulse buys wins, and the savings account remains untouched. We are masters of agreement but slaves to inaction.

It is the paradox of human nature—our minds can grasp complex truths, but our actions remain shackled by emotion, fear, and inertia. This is not just a financial issue; it is a fundamental struggle of existence. We are creatures of comfort, drawn to the familiar, hesitant to embrace the unknown.

***

We seek validation instead of action. When faced with a dilemma, I become a knowledge sponge. I consult friends, family, experts—anyone who might offer insight. I listen intently, nodding along, agreeing with their points. But here's the kicker: I rarely follow their advice. More often than not, I end up choosing the path I was leaning toward all along.

So why bother asking? Because deep down, I'm searching for that one missing piece, that overlooked detail that will validate my gut feeling or illuminate a hidden risk. I'm chasing the illusion of certainty—the hope that someone will articulate the very thought I haven't quite grasped yet.

And here's the brutal truth: most of the time, that epiphany never comes. But in the process of listening, I find myself agreeing with points I've already considered. "Man has no ears for what he already knows," Nietzsche aptly observed. We mistake familiarity for novelty, believing we've stumbled upon a groundbreaking idea when, in reality, it's merely a reflection of our own subconscious reasoning.

We seek comfort in agreement because action is uncomfortable. Agreement is easy; execution is hard. It requires effort, risk, and commitment—things our mind resists instinctively. This pattern applied to my financial journey as well. During my time at startups, Indian MNCs, and later in the US, I listened to countless colleagues discuss investment strategies—some swore by aggressive stock market plays, others advocated safe, long-term funds. But did I follow their advice? Not really. I took an unconventional approach. Instead of carefully planned investments, I simply parked my money in an account and pretended it didn't exist. I was saving, but without any structured investment strategy.

Did this approach cost me? Absolutely. One of my biggest financial regrets was not opting for a 401(k)-retirement plan for the first five years in the US. I had access to free money through employer contributions, yet I ignored it. I also failed to invest in stocks when companies like Apple, Amazon, Microsoft, and Google had shares ranging between $20 and $45. Had I taken action then, my financial standing today would be vastly different. But hesitation— driven by fear and lack of exploration—held me back.

***

Fear is the invisible barrier. This phenomenon is particularly prevalent in finance. We watch a video about a new investment strategy, and it resonates. "This makes perfect sense," we think. "I should try this." But then, fear creeps in. It's an uncharted territory, a step into the unknown. What if it fails? What if I lose money? The comfort of the familiar, even if it's stagnant, feels safer than the potential of the unexplored.

Consider this: A fresh graduate, earning □25,000 per month, can easily save □2,000. It's a small sacrifice, just 8% of their income. Yet, for many, it feels insurmountable. Why? Because after 22 years of financial dependence, the newfound freedom of earning feels intoxicating. The urge to spend, to indulge, to finally experience the fruits of their labor, overrides the logic of saving.

This is the Action Gap in its most basic form. You can do it, but you choose not to. It's not about capability; it's about mindset.

And isn't this the story of our lives? How often do we let fear dictate our choices? How often do we know what's best for us, yet fail to act? The mind, despite its infinite capacity for logic, is still governed by primal instincts—the fear of loss, the aversion to pain, the preference for immediate gratification.

***

Most financial discussions are one-sided. We consume information passively—watching a video, reading an article, listening to a podcast. We nod along, agree with the points, and then move on. There's no engagement, no active participation, no internalization of the message. It's like pouring water into a leaky bucket—it seeps out as quickly as it goes in.

We need to shift from passive consumption to active engagement. Stop treating financial advice as entertainment and start treating it as a roadmap. Move from "I agree" to "I act." Knowledge without execution is empty. Wisdom lies in execution. The sages of history did not sit in their chambers merely contemplating life; they acted upon their insights. The same applies to us.

***

The solution, though simple in theory, requires a fundamental shift in mindset: Do not do anything that doesn't add value to your life. This is the thumb rule, the guiding principle that should govern every decision.

But what does value mean? It's subjective, of course. For some, it's financial security. For others, it's time freedom. For still others, it's the ability to pursue their passions. But whatever your definition, your actions should align with it.

Let's face it: in today's world, you either inherit wealth or build it. For most of us, the latter is the only option. And building wealth requires action, not just agreement. It requires a clear vision, a well-defined plan, and the courage to step outside our comfort zones.

***

Here's the real question: Are you living your life, or are you living the life someone else has prescribed for you? Are you making choices based on your own values and aspirations, or are you succumbing to societal pressures and expectations?

The Action Gap is not just about money—it's about mindset, agency, and life itself. It's about surrendering your agency, relinquishing control over your own destiny. It's about settling for mediocrity when you're capable of greatness.

***

The time for agreement is over. The time for action is now. Start small. Take one step, however insignificant it may seem: Open a savings account. Invest a small amount. Create a budget to start with. The key is to break the cycle of inaction, to prove to yourself that you are capable of change. Don't wait for the perfect moment, the perfect plan, the perfect opportunity. They don't exist. Start where you are, with what you have, and build from there.

Remember, your life is not a spectator sport. You're not here to watch others succeed; you're here to create your own success story. Bridge the Action Gap, and you'll unlock a world of possibilities—a future where your dreams become your reality.

***

Chapter 2: Relentless Learning and Self-Investment

"The man who does not value himself, cannot value anything or anyone." – Ayn Rand

A salaried-class life often revolves around work—more work, impressing the boss, earning, and making ends meet. But have you ever noticed how even what we do outside of work still somehow ties back to it? Why? Because work provides shelter, food, and clothing. It's a survival mindset. Breaking out of this cycle isn't easy unless we slowly but steadily build wealth. But how do we do that when we dedicate 15–18 hours a day to work-related activities, including travel and preparation? By the time we return home, exhaustion sets in, and all we crave is peace.

There must be a way out—because every problem, eventually, has a solution.

***

The journey of continuous learning is the key to a better financial prospect. Right after college, I made a decision: every single day, I would learn something new. Not a day has passed since my graduation that I haven't learned at least one thing. It started with my enrollment in a CCNA certification course (Cisco Certified Network Associate). To attend weekday morning classes, I traveled 40 km one way. I didn't take the certification exam, but I learned the concepts.

Next, I joined an MCSA certification course (Microsoft Certified Systems Administrator), which I attended on weekends. This time, I got certified because my startup job required these concepts daily. Then came my decision to prepare for GRE, which required even more dedication. The GRE classes were held every Saturday and Sunday, 50 km away from my home. The schedule was intense: Math from 9 AM to 11.30 AM, English from 2 PM to 5 PM.

Since the institute allowed unlimited attendance for 1.5 years, I took full advantage of it—I never missed a single class.

However, there was a major challenge: English. Though I had studied in schools with English as the medium, the instructor had an American accent, making it incredibly difficult to follow. For the first month (eight classes), I couldn't understand a full sentence. Still, I persevered. During the break between Math and English, instead commuting, I would sit in the scorching Chennai heat at the beach until 1:30 PM, waiting for the next class to begin.

This phase of my life instilled in me an unexpected passion: reading books. Since my startup had fewer work tickets due to a small team of 30 people, I used office hours to develop a habit of reading books. This not only improved my English but also inspired me to write a book titled *The Great Confusion*—an autobiography about my struggles after graduation. Unfortunately, I lost it when my office computer crashed.

Did I attempt the GRE? Yes. I scored 960/1600, with a higher score in English than in Math. But in the end, I didn't pursue a master's degree abroad due to financial constraints and my decision not to burden my parents further.

***

I learnt from every opportunity. My first Indian MNC job wasn't in my area of expertise (networking, firewalls, antivirus) but in performance testing. Training and projects took me to Chennai, Hyderabad, and Delhi. But more than the technical aspects, I absorbed corporate culture, client communication, email etiquette, reporting, and professional presentations. My mentor and team lead played a crucial role in shaping me. He was a workaholic, and naturally, I became one too. Many nights, we would sleep in the office dormitory in Hyderabad rather than go home after a long tiring day at work.

When the project ended, we moved to Delhi, where we lived in a company-sponsored guesthouse for nearly nine months, costing □1,500 per person per day. Since I was stationed at the client's office, I observed how high-level communication and presentations worked.

When my mentor decided to leave for an international MNC, I followed suit. Thanks to his guidance, I was able to answer all but one question in my interview. His influence went beyond work—he would ask me every single day, *"What did you learn today?"* If my answer was *"nothing,"* I had to endure a long lecture that followed. His persistence ensured I never stopped learning.

***

At my new job in my first International MNC, I had more free time in the first few months. That's when I grew close to someone-my roommate's cousin. I got introduced to her by my roommate when I was in ISRO - Indian Space Research Organization for my Engineering project in the final year of my graduation. She later moved abroad for her master's degree and inspired me to prepare for GRE. Though I didn't go abroad, she influenced me in another way—she was learning French to secure a Canadian PR. Seeing her approach, I did the same and joined weekend French classes for 2.5 years at Alliance Française de Madras until I moved to the US. I completed three levels of certification classes but secured level 2 certification (DELF A2) since I never attempted A3, despite attending the classes.

Even today, I continue learning. As of June 2025, I have been using Duolingo for 1050 consecutive days to improve my French. Before going to bed, I also make it a habit to read at least 10 pages of a book, regardless of the genre.

***

“He who has a why to live can bear almost any how.” – Friedrich Nietzsche

Entertainment can be educational if used wisely. While YouTube is often seen as a distraction, it is also a source of high-quality content. I even uploaded short 15-second videos daily about what I eat every morning. Earlier, my spouse and I had a YouTube channel dedicated to cooking videos, which we ran for three years, uploading 150 videos while in the US.

Though we eventually stopped due to limited financial returns, I don’t regret a second of it—I gained hands-on skills in shooting, editing, and content creation.

Yes, I was being selfish-but about my growth. The point is simple: No one will take care of you—you must. The world is a race. No one else will lose sleep if you fail; they are focused on their own success. If you don’t realize this early, you risk being left behind. However, I am not saying you should follow my path. Everyone’s journey is different. But one thing is universal: learn something new every day. The goal is not just knowledge—it is financial progress through learning.

Try different avenues, learn to invest for your future, and always put your growth first. Be selfish about your growth. Be frugal with your choices. That’s how you build not just wealth—but freedom.

***

Chapter 3. The Credit Card Trap

"Beware of little expenses; a small leak will sink a great ship." – Benjamin Franklin

The moment you land your first job, your company sets up a salary account—and soon after, the bank makes its next move—offering you a credit card. It feels like a rite of passage into financial adulthood—sleek, empowering, and deceptively convenient. And most people, without a second thought, accept it.

Why wouldn't they? The glossy brochures, the lucrative offers, the cashback rewards, the "spend now, pay later" convenience—it all seems so perfect. But reality is far from what these credit card evangelists preach. They highlight the best-case scenarios, showing you the perks, the benefits, the privileges. What they conveniently ignore is the worst-case scenario, the real side of credit card debt—the one where financial mismanagement leads to a spiral of repayments, interest, and stress.

***

Having a credit card in your wallet creates an illusion of wealth. You don't feel the pinch of spending because everything happens in a swipe. You start making impulse purchases—things you don't need, things you'd hesitate to buy if you were handing over your hard-earned cash.

The usual mindset is, *Let's worry about it when the bill arrives.* But by the time it does, you've already dug a hole too deep to climb out of easily.

One of the biggest mistakes people make is misunderstanding the concept of minimum payments. Banks allow you to pay just a fraction of the total bill, and it feels like an easy way out. But here's the trap—whatever remains unpaid starts accumulating interest at an alarmingly high rate, sometimes even more than a personal loan. Before you know it, you're stuck in an endless loop of paying off old dues while continuing to spend on new ones.

"You cannot escape the responsibility of tomorrow by evading it today." – Abraham Lincoln

This is exactly what happens when people rely on minimum payments. They push the burden forward, thinking they'll manage it next month. But next month brings its own expenses, and the cycle continues.

***

I was no exception. When I got my first credit card, it was through my bank at my first international MNC job.

Did I make the same mistakes as everyone else? No.

Did I know everything about credit cards back then? Absolutely not.

So why didn't I fall into the trap? Simple: I hate owing money. Any amount of money owed to someone else—even a small sum—feels like a burden to me. And a good night's sleep is priceless.

When choosing a card, I opted for an Indian Oil credit card, which gave me points every time I refueled my vehicle. Since I was commuting 60 km daily, this card made sense. The points I earned were redeemed for movie ticket vouchers—a small but useful perk.

Did I use the credit card for other expenses? No.

I restricted its use to fixed expenses—internet bills, phone bills, and nothing beyond that. The card offered more perks, but I deliberately ignored them. Why? Because the moment you start exploring "offers," you start spending on things you never needed in the first place. And once you fall into that trap, there is no easy way out.

***

When I moved to the US, I was told that building a credit score is crucial if I planned to live there long-term. It was emphasized so much that it felt like an absolute necessity.

So, what did I do? I got a credit card.

Did I build a credit score? Yes. And not just any score—I built an exceptionally high credit score, something only a small percentage of people achieve.

But here’s where my experience differed from most others:

- I never used my credit card beyond what I could afford.
- My US credit card was geared toward shopping rewards, but instead of falling into a spending spree, I converted my reward points into dollars, redeemable for anything once I met a minimum limit.
- Most importantly, I created a monthly budget at the start of each month, ensuring I was always in control of my spending.

***

I made a firm choice: No more credit cards—no matter the perks. I had seen enough. I had understood the system. I had experienced firsthand how easy it is to slip, even when you think you're being careful. The convenience of credit cards often disguises the real cost—one small misstep, and you’re caught in a cycle of debt that keeps growing.

That’s why I knew I had to stop. Owning multiple cards only makes things worse. Managing different accounts, tracking due dates, and keeping up with ever-changing interest rates is a mental load most people underestimate. Before you know it, you’re not just spending money—you’re losing control of it. And that’s a risk I was no longer willing to take.

***

Over the years, I developed a few rules for myself—rules that ensured I never fell victim to the credit card debt trap. These are principles that anyone can follow:

Know your expenses before swiping – Never use a credit card without knowing in advance how much you will have to pay at the end of the month.

Use credit cards only for fixed expenses – Bills that are necessary and non-negotiable (e.g., internet, electricity) are fine. Impulse purchases? Absolutely not.

Never spend beyond your means – If you earn $4,000 per month and your usual expenses are $2,500, you have a surplus of $1,500. If you spend more than that on your credit card, you are setting yourself up for disaster.

This is just an example and I would never advocate this.

Just because you have credit limit, doesn't mean you should use it – A credit limit of $10,000 doesn't mean you have $10,000 to spend. That's the bank's money, not yours.

Debt is not free money – Every penny borrowed has to be repaid, often with interest that makes it far more expensive than you realize.

"Debt is like any other trap, easy enough to get into, but hard enough to get out of." – Henry Wheeler Shaw. And banks have perfected the art of baiting that trap.

***

Credit cards are not evil. They are tools. But just like a sharp knife, if you don't know how to use them properly, you'll end up hurting yourself.

Banks make billions by convincing people to spend money they don't have, on things they don't need, and then charge them interest for the privilege. The only way to win this game is not to play—or if you must, to play by your own rules and never theirs.

Use credit wisely, or better yet, don't use it at all.

A debt-free life is a stress-free life. And nothing—no amount of reward points, cashback offers, or so-called perks—is worth losing your peace of mind over.

***

Chapter 4 - Loans from Friends

Having a friend feels like bliss. The comfort of knowing someone is always there for you—especially in times of financial need—feels almost divine. But remember, this privilege often has an expiration date. The moment life responsibilities shift, priorities change, and the unwavering support you once relied on may not be as readily available anymore.

Marriage is a pivotal shift. Suddenly, personal freedom becomes shared responsibility. Financial decisions aren't made in isolation anymore—they involve spouses, families, futures. It's not personal; it's just how life works. The friend who once generously covered your expenses without a second thought may suddenly insist on splitting the bill. It's not that they don't care—it's that they now have to care about more than just you.

Friendship thrives on emotional support, shared laughter, and guidance through life's ups and downs. But the moment money enters the equation, it introduces a complexity that can turn even the strongest of bonds into fragile arrangements.

"Blessed is he who expects nothing, for he shall never be disappointed." – Alexander Pope.

The biggest disappointments in friendships often stem from unmet expectations. Every financial favor you expect from a friend puts a hairline crack in your bond. Enough cracks, and even steel will snap.

***

When I started working for my first multinational company, I made it a rule to budget at the beginning of each month. Despite my best efforts, I frequently found myself running low on cash by the 15th or 20th. I had my reasons, which I will detail in later chapters. But rather than tapping into my savings, I had a system—I borrowed small amounts, around 2,000–3,000 INR, from a colleague with the promise of repaying on salary day. It became a routine, almost a monthly ritual.

I made it a point to clear my dues immediately upon receiving my paycheck. Since my colleague knew my track record of prompt repayment, there was never a problem. But let's consider a different scenario—what if I missed a payment? What if, one month, I failed to return the money on time? The dynamic would shift. The ease with which I borrowed before would vanish, replaced by hesitation, unspoken tension, and the possibility of a refusal the next time I needed help. That's the danger: one delayed payment, and trust erodes—not loudly, but silently, like a leak you don't notice until it's too late.

***

There was another instance when I borrowed a much larger sum—26,000 INR—from a different colleague. He came from a financially comfortable background, just like my usual lender, and the principle remained the same: repay on salary day. Everything went smoothly, but what if I had failed to pay him back? Would our camaraderie have survived? Or would he start viewing me not as a friend but as a liability?

***

When I moved to the US, a similar situation arose, but on a larger scale. Nine months in, I needed to buy a car. I had been planning for it, saving up, but when the moment came, I fell short by $2,000. The car's final cost was around $8,600. I could have taken a loan from my employer, but that meant a deduction of $250 from every paycheck until the amount was cleared. Instead, I turned to my manager.

His response was eye-opening. He said, "It wasn't about the money. It was about risk. Risk to rapport. Risk to reputation. And in a professional setting, that risk is never worth it." I understood his reasoning immediately. It wasn't about his financial capability—it was about preserving a working relationship. Money has the power to corrode even professional bonds, not just friendships.

Eventually, I borrowed the amount from a colleague. Not only did he lend me the money, but he also helped me test-drive the vehicle, accompanied me to the dealership, and even drove the car home after purchase. His generosity extended beyond financial assistance—he played a crucial role in the entire process.

I had agreed to a repayment plan: $1,000 in October, nothing in November (since Thanksgiving meant a lot of tempting shopping deals), and the final $1,000 in December.

During those months, he would casually ask, "How's the car?" Not frequently, but enough times to make me wonder if it was his way of reminding me about the debt. My spouse certainly thought so. Money changes context. A kind question becomes a subtle reminder. Intentions blur. That's the power of debt—it rewires how we hear people.

Her interpretation was: "He's reminding you to pay him back."

Was she right? Possibly. Was he merely asking out of curiosity? Maybe. But this is the uncertainty that money introduces into relationships—it changes the way we interpret even the most casual of conversations.

I made sure to clear my dues by end of November, eliminating any potential discomfort between us.

"Before borrowing money from a friend, it's best to decide which you need most." – Joe Moore

***

In India, the definition of a "friend" is broad. Anyone you know, you often refer to as a "friend." But when it comes to borrowing money, a distinction must be made. A friend is someone who supports you, but the moment money is involved, they become a lender. And a lender—no matter how close—will always expect repayment.

Money can build or break relationships. It has the power to shift dynamics, alter perceptions, and introduce unspoken resentments. Borrow wisely, and more importantly, borrow cautiously.

This is not an endorsement of borrowing money from friends or borrowing in the first place. If anything, it is a warning. If you must borrow, be prepared for the consequences. Choose wisely, and more importantly, repay diligently.

"If borrowing is unavoidable, let your integrity—not convenience—dictate your actions." – I don't remember who said this—but it's a principle worth living by.

***

Chapter 5 - Differentiate Spending

A Multi-Account Approach to Financial Discipline

"It is not the man who has little, but he who desires more, that is poor." – Seneca

Human desires are unlimited. We always want more. The moment we see a lump sum amount in our bank account, there is an instinctive urge to spend. For most people, seeing a big paycheck at the end of the month feels like a well-earned reward, and rightfully so. But the real reward is in how we manage that money.

This is where differentiating spending becomes crucial.

Imagine this: you work hard all month and receive your salary. The money comes in, and soon, various expenses start eating into it—monthly bills, rent, EMIs (if applicable), groceries, medical expenses, and so on. Everything gets deducted from the same salary account, making it difficult to track and plan efficiently.

When all your money sits in one place, every purchase feels affordable. Differentiated accounts impose mental boundaries. They create the illusion of scarcity, which forces discipline. Instead, having multiple bank accounts can help you differentiate and manage your finances better.

***

Instead of using your salary account for all transactions, you can budget at the start of the month and distribute funds to different accounts based on their purpose. Here's how:

- Salary Account: Keep your salary here but do not use it for day-to-day expenses.
- Spending Account: Transfer the necessary amount for monthly spending.
- Savings Account: Allocate a portion to long-term savings.
- Investment Account: Keep funds for stock trading, mutual funds, or other investments.

This way, your salary account is not exposed to frequent transactions, making tracking and planning easier.

***

Over the years, through different phases of my career, I accumulated multiple bank accounts due to job changes and financial decisions. Let me take you through my journey:

Phase 1: The Initial Days – Bank A

My first salary account was with Bank A, as it was the designated bank of my first employer. At this stage, all my expenses and savings were in one place. A basic setup, but not the most efficient.

Phase 2: Startup Life – Bank B & Bank C

When I joined a startup, my salary was transferred to Bank B. After a couple of years, the company switched to Bank C for salary deposits.

At this stage, I now had:

- Bank A – Dormant but still open.
- Bank B – Salary account.
- Bank C – New salary account.

Phase 3: First Indian MNC – Bank D

Upon moving to an Indian MNC, another account was opened—Bank D. By now, I had four accounts:

1. Bank A – Dormant.
2. Bank B – No longer receiving salary.
3. Bank C – Not used.
4. Bank D – Active salary account.

Phase 4: International MNC – Structured Allocation

When I moved to an international MNC, I was allowed to choose my preferred bank, and I opted for Bank D again. Now, with a structured salary, I devised the following allocation plan:

- Almost 50% transferred to Bank B – This bank had a feature where unused funds were automatically moved to a fixed deposit (FD) at a high interest rate.

- Bank D Credit Card for Fixed Bills – Internet, mobile, fuel, etc.
- Clear the load to my lender colleague.
- 15% for Home Maintenance – Sent to my parents every month via Bank D.
- 7% Auto-Debit to a Food Card – This was a tax-free benefit provided by the company, reducing taxable income while ensuring a dedicated food budget. The amount was deducted from my salary before tax calculations, meaning I saved money while having a predefined allocation for meals.
- Remaining amount in Bank D for flexible spending - Usually untouched

To ensure better control, I handed over my Bank B debit card to my mom and chose to "forget" about it, treating it as a long-term savings account. Over time, this strategy led to the accumulation of multiple Fixed Deposits (CoDs) in Bank B.

Phase 5: The US Transition – Bank D in Action

When I moved to the US, Bank D became my primary account for sending monthly funds home. The structured approach ensured my finances were on track despite the relocation.

Phase 6: Return to India – Bank C as the Daily Driver

Upon returning to India and joining another Indian MNC in a different city, Bank D remained my salary account, but the usage changed. Instead of using it for expenses, I redirected it only to distribute funds towards other banks. Bank C was activated to serve as my daily expense account, ensuring that my salary was not directly exposed to numerous transactions. This segregation helped me maintain better control over spending while keeping a clear record of where my money was going.

- Bank C Activated – Now serves as my daily expense account.
- Bank C Debit Card with Parents – For their expenses.
- UPI for My Transactions – Making daily payments seamless.
- Bank B for Investments – Used for stock trading and long-term investments.
- Bank A Still Dormant – However, it continues to accrue interest each quarter.

***

Setting up multiple bank accounts isn't about complicating things—it's about bringing clarity, control, and security to your finances. By segmenting money based on purpose, you prevent unnecessary spending, ensure consistent savings, and make tracking finances much easier. This structure also builds financial discipline, as you are less likely to dip into funds allocated for savings or investments. Furthermore, keeping separate accounts provides security in case of fraud or unexpected issues with any single bank. On the other hand, failing to differentiate your spending leads to chaos—money comes in and goes out without a clear plan, making it difficult to save, invest, or even track where your hard-earned income is going. Without structured financial planning, there is a higher risk of overspending, liquidity issues, and missed investment opportunities, ultimately leading to financial stress and instability.

"Do not save what is left after spending, but spend what is left after saving." – Warren Buffett

Your takeaway system:

1 Salary Account (inflow only)

1 Expense Account (monthly spend)

1 Long-term Savings (FDs, emergency fund)

1 Investment Account (stocks, mutual funds)

Optional: 1 Family Account (for parents/spouse)

***

Chapter 6 - Minimalistic Living

"You never know what is enough unless you know what is more than enough." - William Blake

We live in a world where people equate success with possessions. The more we own, the more accomplished we feel. But in doing so, we often sacrifice happiness, financial security, and peace of mind.

What do we truly need in life? Food, shelter, and clothing—nothing more, nothing less. At its core, life is simple. But to acquire even these basics, we need money, a construct we humans created, just like we created the concept of God. And in the pursuit of this money, we are all caught in an endless rat race—chasing, earning, spending, and then chasing again.

Money is a tool meant to help us meet our needs, yet paradoxically, for many, it has become the very reason for existence. We work tirelessly to earn, and then we spend excessively—often on things we don't need. This is the paradox of modern life.

But what do I mean by "things we don't need"? Look around you. How often do you buy something just because it is trending on Instagram? How frequently do you purchase items not out of necessity, but because a friend has them, or because marketing convinced you that you need them? People still buy the new iPhone for no reason when their old one is still functional.

This cycle of consumption is endless, and the reasons behind it are just as infinite.

***

We need to define "Need" in a world of excess. What does a family of three truly require?

- Nutritious food.
- A comfortable and safe place to live.
- Clothing to present ourselves decently.
- Basic utilities like electricity, transportation, phone, and gas bills.

Beyond these, most other expenses are discretionary. Yet, society conditions us to believe otherwise. The difference between necessity and luxury is not always clear-cut—it is often dictated by our perspective.

For instance, consider the following questions:

- Do we truly need 100 Mbps internet when you know that 40–50 Mbps is sufficient?
- Is a 2-ton AC necessary when a 1-ton AC would suffice?
- Does a family require a 55-inch television, or would a 40-inch screen serve the same purpose?
- Do we need a 7-seater couch when a 4-seater with extra chairs would work?

- Is an SUV necessary when a smaller, fuel-efficient car is enough?
- How many clothes do we truly need?
- How many items in our home are rarely, if ever, used?

The answers to these questions are subjective, of course. We live in a democracy, and everyone has the right to choose their lifestyle. But this book is about the philosophy of money, and financial discipline is exactly what I am trying to highlight.

***

If we look at nature, animals live in the most minimalistic way possible. A bird does not build a palace to live in; it creates a small nest just enough to keep itself and its young safe. A lion does not hunt more than it can eat. A deer does not collect grass for the next ten years. Animals live only with what they need. They do not hoard. Some do, but only for survival, not for social status. They live in a way that is in balance with nature. But humans, despite being the most intelligent species, complicate life with unnecessary possessions and material desires. Instead of living for survival and happiness, we live for comparison and social validation. And in that process, we forget to actually live.

***

Happiness is a choice. The world is a place where a person earning $500 a month can live happily, just as much as a person earning $5000 a month. At the same time, a person with $5000 may not be happy because of his choices. It all comes down to how one manages their resources and what they prioritize. The person earning $500 may live in a small home, cook simple meals, and find joy in relationships and experiences rather than things. Meanwhile, the person earning $5000 may be drowning in loans, trapped by lifestyle inflation, and constantly chasing the next expensive thing, thinking it will bring happiness. The truth is, happiness is not in how much money you make but in how wisely you use it.

A simple life, free from unnecessary financial burdens, is often the most peaceful and fulfilling one. The ability to say 'no' to excess and 'yes' to what truly matters is the key to financial well-being and personal contentment.

***

Look at some of the most successful people in the world—Steve Jobs, who wore the same black turtleneck and blue jeans every day; Mark Zuckerberg, who sticks to his simple gray T-shirt. They are billionaires, yet their choices reflect minimalism. Why? Because they understand that time and energy are finite. By reducing trivial decisions like what to wear, they free up their minds for more meaningful pursuits.

Living simply doesn't mean deprivation; it means prioritization. It means consciously choosing what truly adds value to our lives and eliminating the rest.

***

A cluttered home reflects a cluttered mind. Imagine living in a house packed with unused items—drawers overflowing with clothes you don't wear, kitchen shelves lined with gadgets you rarely use, decorative pieces gathering dust. It not only creates chaos but also drains mental energy. The more things you own, the more you must clean, maintain, and worry about. Contrast this with a home that contains only what is needed—a home where every item serves a purpose. Such an environment fosters peace, clarity, and efficiency.

The "Three-Times-a-Week" rule: When I lived in the US, my spouse and I made a simple pact: We would not buy anything unless we were sure it would be used at least three times a month. This single rule saved us a fortune and kept our home clutter-free. I'm grateful to my spouse for supporting me in this journey.

We continued this practice even after moving into our new home. As a result, our 1,250-square-foot house feels incredibly spacious. My child and I can play cricket in the living room or even turn it into a makeshift bowling alley. Instead of crowding the space with excess furniture, we own only the essentials—no dining table, no coffee table, no bedside tables, no unnecessary décor. Just what we truly need. The result? Peace of mind, fewer financial burdens, and a sense of freedom. There's room to breathe, to move, to live. After all, a home is meant to be a sanctuary, not a dumping ground for unwanted things.

***

Every item we purchase comes with two costs:

1. The cost of buying it.
2. The cost of maintaining it.

The financial strain of purchasing things we don't need is obvious, but the mental burden is often overlooked. When we buy more, we need bigger spaces, more maintenance, and increased responsibilities. The more we own, the more we are owned by our possessions.

Minimalism as a financial strategy. Minimalism is not about deprivation—it is about making conscious choices. Before purchasing something, ask yourself:

- Will this add value to my life or just to my lifestyle?
- Will this serve a meaningful purpose, or is it just a momentary desire?
- Can I function just as well without it?

By adopting this mindset, we not only remove clutter but also free up time, mental space, and most importantly—money.

Letting go of material possessions is liberating. It shifts our focus from "owning more" to "experiencing more." The less we are attached to objects, the more we can invest in meaningful relationships, personal growth, and financial stability.

***

The essence of minimalism is captured beautifully in the words of Hans Hofmann: *"The ability to simplify means to eliminate the unnecessary so that the necessary may speak."*

By choosing to live with less, we gain more—more time, more clarity, more peace. And in doing so, we create a life that is not just financially secure, but also truly fulfilling.

Minimalism is not about having nothing. It is about having exactly what you need—and nothing more.

***

Minimalism is not an overnight transformation—it's a mindset shift that happens over time. The key is to be intentional with your choices. Here are some practical steps to help you transition from a cluttered life to a minimalist one:

Take a deep look at everything you own. Go through your wardrobe, kitchen, and living space, and ask yourself:

- Do I use this regularly?
- Does this add real value to my life?

- Am I keeping this out of guilt or habit? Anything that does not serve a purpose or bring you joy is clutter. Let go of it.

For every new item you bring into your home, get rid of one. This keeps your possessions in check and prevents accumulation. For example, if you are buying a new refrigerator, the old one should no longer exist in your home. Exchange it or discard it.

Commit to removing one unnecessary item from your home every day for a month. By the end of 30 days, you will have eliminated 30 things you don't need. You'll realize how much excess you were holding onto without even noticing.

We accumulate papers, books, receipts, and other documents that take up space. Consider scanning important papers and switching to digital formats for books, magazines, and notes.

Instead of spending money on material things, invest in experiences—travel, learning new skills, or spending quality time with loved ones. The memories created will be far more fulfilling than any possession.

Limit exposure to ads and marketing influences. Unfollow brands that constantly tempt you to buy things you don't need. Be mindful of impulse buying—pause before making any purchase and ask yourself if it's truly necessary.

The goal is not to live with nothing but to live with enough. Start small, stay consistent, and watch how minimalism transforms your life—financially, mentally, and emotionally.

Chapter 7: Lifestyle Inflation

Wealth is the product of man's capacity to think," said Ayn Rand. A fitting observation. It encapsulates the driving force behind human ambition and progress. This isn't merely about intellectual prowess; it's about the application of rational thought to our financial decisions. We must critically evaluate investment options, challenge conventional wisdom, and design a financial strategy that aligns with our individual goals, not just societal expectations. We strive, we push boundaries, and we sacrifice—often more than we realize—all in pursuit of a better life. The irony, however, lies in the fact that despite all our efforts to secure the future, many of us end up trapped in an unending cycle of consumption.

At the core of this cycle is lifestyle inflation—an almost invisible force that creeps into our lives the moment we start earning more. We work hard, land a higher-paying job, and relish the achievement. The pay raise feels like a reward for our dedication, a tangible recognition of our progress. There is nothing inherently wrong with indulging in a few well-earned luxuries. The issue arises when increased income leads to proportional or even excessive increases in spending, often on things we once considered unnecessary.

What happens next is predictable. The euphoria of a pay raise fades, but the new spending habits persist. A larger house, a flashier car, the latest gadgets—none of these are essential, yet they begin to feel like necessities. Society normalizes this behavior. It expects visible signs of success. The bigger house and the expensive car aren't just personal choices anymore; they become a statement—a way to signal one's status to peers.

But here's the real question: If you could live comfortably before, why can't you continue living the same way after the pay raise? What purpose does the spending serve? Is it genuine need or merely the mindless pursuit of external validation?

***

Nietzsche once said, "All interpretations of reality are inherently subjective" a statement that forces us to confront the fact that our understanding of 'value' is not absolute. This is especially true for money. Our interpretation of what we need versus what we want is shaped by external influences—advertisements, peer pressure, and societal expectations. The financial industry thrives on lifestyle inflation. Banks eagerly offer loans with attractive interest rates, credit card companies tempt us with rewards, and advertisements subtly make us feel inadequate without the latest version of something we already own. This is by design fueled by a subjective interpretation of success that is often at odds with true financial well-being. The more we spend, the more money circulates in the economy, benefiting corporations, financial institutions, and the government. But does it truly benefit us?

Think about it. Why do we convince ourselves that an upgrade is necessary when the old version works just fine? Why does an iPhone from two years ago suddenly feel outdated when a new model is launched? Is it because it has genuinely become inefficient, or because we have been conditioned to believe that newer is always better? The truth is, most of our purchases are driven not by necessity but by an inability to resist impulse and external influence.

***

I recall when I bought my first motorcycle. I had just switched to my first international MNC, and my paycheck had increased significantly. Naturally, many assumed I would opt for a premium model. A friend, who had experience purchasing bikes for himself and his extended family, insisted I should go for a higher-end version. "Why settle for less when you can afford more?" he reasoned.

But I held my ground. I didn't buy the bike because I had extra money—I bought it because I needed it. Though public transportation was available for my weekend classes, it would have cost me two to three hours of precious time—something I couldn't afford to lose. Time is the only resource we can never earn back. By choosing to spend my money on something that gave me back those hours, I was making an investment in myself. Over the course of a year, this translated to saving approximately 600-700 hours, equivalent to nearly a month of full-time work, which I could then reinvest into personal development and leisure. That motorcycle has served me faithfully through job changes, relocations, and life transitions. Even as my paychecks increased, I consciously chose to maintain it, recognizing its enduring value. It still serves me well.

Similarly, when I moved to the US, I needed a car. Instead of opting for an expensive financing option, I took a loan from a colleague and cleared it in a couple of months. Remember? That car served me until the very evening before my return flight home. I wasn't attached to it as a status symbol—it was a functional tool that fulfilled its purpose. That's the essence of mindful spending.

Over the past fifteen years, I have owned only four mobile phones. Not because I couldn't afford more, but because I didn't see the need. One of those phones was replaced only because it was damaged in a bike accident. I've often been tempted—whether by GoPros, Chromebooks, or the latest Pixel devices—but in each case, logic prevailed over impulse. Even being an ardent fan of Google and its products, did not win me over to spend on them unnecessarily. My spouse's support played a crucial role in reinforcing these rational choices. By resisting the urge to upgrade every year, I've likely saved several thousand dollars, which, when compounded over time, significantly contributes to long-term financial stability.

Am I boasting? No. Am I justifying my choices? Hardly. I am merely sharing a philosophy—one that prioritizes rationality over impulse. These choices, though seemingly small, have compounded over time, allowing me to accelerate my journey towards financial goals. Each saved hour, each avoided interest payment, and each resisted upgrade has been a deliberate step towards building a life of greater freedom and control.

***

The truth is, money in itself is neutral. It is a tool—nothing more, nothing less. What makes it powerful is how we use it. Used wisely, it provides security, freedom, and opportunities. Squandered mindlessly, it becomes a source of stress, entrapment, and regret.

Being financially independent isn't about making more money; it's about making smarter choices. It's about understanding that true wealth is not in how much you earn, but in how much control you have over your resources.

Many people assume that self-discipline with money means depriving oneself. But in reality, it is the opposite. It is about prioritizing what truly matters—health, time, experiences, and peace of mind—over fleeting pleasures and external validation.

The problem with lifestyle inflation is that it places people on a perpetual treadmill. The more they earn, the more they spend, and the more they feel the need to earn again to sustain this new lifestyle. It's an endless loop that leaves little room for financial freedom.

***

One of the most underrated yet most empowering financial moves is learning to say no—not to money itself, but to unnecessary spending. It is the ability to recognize when something is a genuine need versus an artificial want. It is about knowing that contentment doesn't come from accumulation but from understanding what truly adds value to your life.

At the end of the day, wealth is not about how much you make—it's about how much you keep and how effectively you use it. Money, when used wisely, is strength. It provides confidence, security, and choices. It allows you to stand on your own, to weather uncertainties, and to pursue what truly matters to you.

Discipline and self-control are not restrictions; they are the foundation of financial independence. And financial independence is not just about having money—it's about having the freedom to make choices without being dictated by circumstances or societal expectations.

"That which does not kill us makes us stronger," said Friedrich Nietzsche. The discipline to resist unnecessary spending, the patience to build wealth strategically, and the wisdom to recognize what truly matters—these are the strengths that lead to genuine financial security.

So, the next time you find yourself tempted to spend on an upgrade, ask yourself: Do I truly need this? Or is this just another instance of lifestyle inflation sneaking into my life?

***

Chapter 8 - Buy Only When You Can Afford in Full

"Check your premises." - Ayn Rand.

People are always in pursuit of happiness, yet they rarely grasp its true essence, its potential impact on their lives, or even its attainability. Their pursuit often transforms into an endless chase for material possessions. As children, they long for a bicycle. In college, they crave a motorbike. Once they land a job, they desire a car. After marriage, they dream of a house. And the list continues, growing relentlessly with age and circumstances.

This is but one perspective. Some people chase after the latest tech, others seek luxury, and many desire branded possessions as status symbols. Then, there are those who are content with what they have. The motivations behind these pursuits vary, but the pattern remains the same.

***

This same flawed thinking extends to financial decisions. When most people decide to buy something, they often lack any logical backing for their decision. To many, money is simply something to be spent. But in reality, money is first a shield—meant to provide safety, stability, and peace of mind—not a shovel for digging deeper into debt. A slight increase in their paycheck leads them to immediately think about how to spend it—rather than how to save or invest it.

Worse, they chase things they can't afford, taking out loans to bridge the gap. I've seen people buying iPhones on EMI (Equated Monthly Installments), homes with home loans, cars with car loans, and even financing their weddings with personal loans. They fall into the EMI trap, enjoying the full benefits of these possessions while carrying the burden of repayment. Most view money as a means to acquire more. But its first purpose is to protect—against uncertainty, against dependency, against fear. They fail to ask a simple question: "Is debt truly a tool for progress, or is it a modern form of enslavement disguised as opportunity? They say a house loan builds an asset, but if you spend half your life working to pay for it, was it really your home—or was it the bank's all along? Does ownership exist if it is conditional?"

Beyond the immediate stress of meeting monthly payments, debt incurs significant costs in the form of interest. These interest payments, often overlooked in the initial excitement of acquiring a new possession, accumulate over time, significantly increasing the overall cost of the item. This hidden cost erodes your wealth, diverting funds that could be used for investments or other financial goals.

The point is not to say that houses, cars, or even loans are unnecessary. Rather, it is about how most people approach these purchases. A home may be necessary, a car may be necessary, and sometimes, a personal loan may be unavoidable. But taking a loan is ultimately a sign of financial insufficiency. If something is done with borrowed money, it either means it is an absolute necessity—or it is a purchase made to satisfy ego.

Most people justify big purchases as progress—but often, it's ego masquerading as confidence. The refusal to update our beliefs—especially about money—is rooted in ego. And that ego often leads to poor financial decisions we don't even recognize as mistakes.

We all are born with an empty mind. Over time, our circumstances, experiences, religious beliefs, and upbringing shape our thought process. At some point, the brain stops accepting new information and convinces itself that whatever it believes is correct. This is the birth of ego. Ego, in this context, is a state of mind where the brain refuses to acknowledge mistakes and correct itself with improved rationale. Once ego takes root, even the strongest rationale fails to convince us otherwise. It creates a barrier, preventing us from seeing the flaws in our thinking. We become blinded by our own convictions, unable to consider alternative perspectives or admit when we are wrong. This is precisely when mistakes are made—mistakes we don't even realize we are making, because our ego convinces us we are right.

This ego-driven mindset is particularly dangerous in financial matters. It can lead us to make impulsive decisions, ignore sound advice, and cling to outdated beliefs. For instance, we might refuse to acknowledge that our investment strategy is flawed or that our spending habits are unsustainable. The ego whispers, 'You know best,' even when the evidence suggests otherwise.

***

My approach is simple: Buy only when you can afford it in full.

This principle grants the luxury of peace of mind, even if it means delaying gratification. If I opt for a loan, I may get what I want instantly. But if I wait, I channel my energy into saving for it, strategizing, and prioritizing. This discipline gives me a sense of purpose and clarity.

Furthermore, avoiding debt grants you unparalleled financial flexibility. Without the burden of monthly payments, you have the freedom to pursue new opportunities, weather unexpected expenses, and adapt to changing circumstances. Debt, on the other hand, creates a rigid financial structure, limiting your options and potentially trapping you in a cycle of repayment.

Remember the motorbike and car I bought? Since the car loan was cleared within a couple of months, I still consider it a lump-sum purchase. The phones I own were bought outright. Every major purchase I've made—including my house—was a lump-sum buy. Some may argue that buying a house with cash is a foolish decision when loans are available at low-interest rates, and the money could instead be invested for higher returns. And they are absolutely right. That was a mistake on my part. I wasn't fully aware of financial optimization strategies back then. I was not well aware of the ways that I could have done this better. Had I invested the full amount into a mutual fund with a Systematic Withdrawal Plan (SWP), the withdrawals could have covered my EMIs while the remaining funds continued to grow. Instead of locking my money into a house, I could have leveraged compounding for greater financial flexibility. I now realize the mistake. But a man can correct his mistakes only if he acknowledges there is one.

***

The core idea remains unchanged: Buy only when you have the full amount. But that doesn't mean you shouldn't be strategic. If you have the cash for a major purchase, you should evaluate whether paying in full is the best option or whether investing elsewhere and managing your funds differently would yield better returns. The key is financial clarity: knowing that you can afford it, knowing that you can pay it back, and knowing that you genuinely need it.

You may have to wait two months, two years, or even a decade—like in the case of buying a home—but the lessons learned during this period will be far more valuable than any academic education. This approach may seem frugal, cruel, or even incompetent in the eyes of those who believe in instant gratification. But as Socrates once said, "The secret of happiness, you see, is not found in seeking more, but in developing the capacity to enjoy less."

This philosophy has worked for me. I endured the long wait. I endured pressure from those around me. I endured occasional arguments. And when the time was right, I made my purchases with confidence, clarity, and absolute ownership. That is true financial freedom.

This freedom is not just about avoiding debt; it's about building a life where your financial decisions are driven by your own goals and values, not by the demands of lenders or the pressure to keep up with societal expectations. Every financial decision is a trade-off between present comfort and future security. You either own your purchases—or they own you. Choose wisely.

***

Chapter 9 - Prepare for the Worst-Case Scenario

"The mind should be sent beforehand to meet the things that threaten it." - Seneca

We all have ambitions, and money plays a crucial role in them. Your ambitions and goals should be the driving force behind everything you do. Every morning when you wake up, there should be a reason—a purpose that fuels your actions. It should not be routine, mundane necessities that push you out of bed, but rather the larger vision you have for your life. And in most cases, achieving that vision requires financial security. While some goals may not demand money, this book is, after all, about financial wisdom. If your own goals cannot motivate you, nothing else can.

Our goals define the purpose of our existence. We aim for something, work toward it, achieve it, and then move on to the next goal. This constant pursuit gives life its momentum. But not everything goes as planned. The unexpected should never come as a rude shock. The way the capitalist world operates is by showing you only one side of the coin—endless possibilities, success stories, and the illusion of stability. The risks, failures, and vulnerabilities are deliberately hidden until they become unavoidable. This is why you must always prepare for the worst-case scenario.

As Seneca rightly said, the mind should anticipate the worst rather than merely await the predictable. Yet most people ignore this principle. They save, spend, and work toward their goals with blind optimism. They do not factor in the unpredictable. Take, for instance, someone buying a car or a house. The obvious choice for most is to take out a loan. If they have a steady income, they assume they can handle the monthly payments. But do they stop to ask: "Can I still pay my EMI if I lose my job tomorrow? Will my family survive without my paycheck?" Or, more critically, "Is my family financially secure if I am no longer around?" The excitement of ownership often blinds people to rational long-term thinking. Most still go ahead, driven by optimism. But what if something goes wrong? This is why preparing for the worst-case scenario is essential.

***

People often mistake worst-case scenario thinking for pessimism. This is a fundamental misunderstanding. Worst-case scenario thinking is not about expecting the worst; it is about preparing for it. It is a proactive approach that provides the mental and financial cushion to withstand shocks. Pessimism, on the other hand, is a passive and defeatist mindset that assumes things will go wrong without seeking solutions.

Consider how businesses operate. Every major corporation runs risk assessments. They plan for worst-case scenarios—market downturns, lawsuits, cybersecurity threats, supply chain disruptions—because they know that ignoring risks can destroy them. Shouldn't individuals do the same for their personal finances?

When you set a financial goal, you do not just focus on achieving it. You also identify obstacles that could derail you. This is the key difference between merely setting a target and strategizing for long-term success. A goal is not just for reaching; it is for aiming with full awareness of possible risks.

***

When I moved to the U.S., I had to choose a medical insurance plan. At the time, I was unmarried, but I knew that within a few months, I would be. I carefully selected a plan that covered all possible scenarios, including an add-on called "voluntary hospitalization." This add-on provided a lump-sum payout for hospital admission and a daily allowance for up to 90 days.

Most people overlook such details, assuming they will be fine with basic coverage. But when we had a baby, this add-on proved invaluable. Our total hospital expenses were around $4,500, yet the insurance payout was $7,500—leaving us financially ahead rather than burdened. This is an example of worst-case scenario planning—not out of fear, but out of foresight. The same logic applies to every aspect of life: work, shopping, spending, investing.

***

Your income is your lifeline. Yet many people take their jobs for granted, assuming their employer will always need them. In reality, companies are constantly adapting, cutting costs, and automating roles. A worst-case thinker prepares by: learning new skills to stay relevant, building a financial buffer in case of sudden job loss, networking and keeping job opportunities open, ensuring their work is future-proof, with clear, valuable contributions.

Even something as simple as sending an email at work should reflect foresight—anticipating potential questions, ensuring clarity, and reducing unnecessary back-and-forth.

People often shop impulsively. They enter a store without a clear plan, get distracted by offers, and end up buying things they do not need. Worst-case scenario thinking eliminates this by: always having a list before shopping, questioning whether each purchase is a want or a need, setting a strict budget to prevent overspending.

When spending on big-ticket items, this mindset is even more critical. Before buying anything expensive, ask: "If I lost my income tomorrow, would this purchase still make sense?" If the answer is no, reconsider.

Many assume that earning more money solves financial problems. But history has repeatedly shown that high incomes without financial preparedness mean nothing. Athletes, celebrities, and lottery winners have all gone bankrupt because they assumed their wealth was limitless.

A worst-case thinker always prepares by: saving at least 6–12 months' worth of expenses, never relying on just one source of income, having health, life, and disability insurances, and diversifying investments. Do not put everything in one asset class.

***

The system is designed to keep you unprepared. Financial institutions do not want you to think about worst-case scenarios. The economy thrives when people spend, borrow, and remain dependent. Banks encourage loans, credit cards push debt, and companies market lifestyle inflation as success.

Look at real estate. People are told, "A house is an asset." But if you spend half your life paying for it, was it really yours—or was it the bank's? Home loans make banks rich, not homeowners.

Similarly, car loans, wedding loans, and EMIs trap people into perpetual financial obligations. By preparing for the worst, you reverse the equation. You gain control. You dictate terms instead of being dictated to.

***

Freedom is in preparation. Baruch Spinoza said, "Freedom is the recognition of necessity." True financial freedom is not about having an endless supply of money—it is about being prepared for life's uncertainties. When you know what you want and work toward it, you must also recognize potential setbacks and plan accordingly.

Worst-case scenario thinking is not about fear. It is about control. The more prepared you are, the less life can surprise you. And when others panic, you remain unshaken—because you saw it coming long before they did.

***

Chapter 10 - Increase Your Salary, Not Your Debts

"Like a camel is man, he kneels down and lets himself be well laden with burdens," said Nietzsche. I read that years ago, and it stuck—a mirror to how we live. Look around: the modern world is a machine driven by the whims of financial institutions. If the government and central banks want more money swirling in the market, they slash interest rates, dangling cheap loans like bait. If they need to curb inflation, they tighten the screws, making capital costly. Either way, the common man—us—takes the hit. We're the camels, kneeling under burdens we didn't design, conditioned to carry more than we should.

Freedom's our instinct. We dream of unshackled lives—no debts, no stress, just peace. But do we act like it? Hardly. When something's cheap, we bought it. When it caught my eye, we grabbed it. When someone flaunted their status, I've felt the tug to keep up. Boredom? We've spent to fill the void. Nietzsche wasn't just philosophizing—he was pointing to our blind spot: we don't feel these burdens until they're crushing us. Spending is destruction, effortless and natural. Saving and investing? That's construction—slow, deliberate, and rare. It's easier to tear down than to build.

***

We've talked about learning as an endless journey (Chapter 2), and investing's no different. Unless you're born with a silver spoon, most of us start small and grow slowly. But what is investing? It's subjective—personal as hell. For some, it is stocks, real estate, gold, even Bitcoin. For others, it's time—learning a skill, nurturing your mind, betting on yourself. I've done both, and they're fair game. The trap opens when we "invest" in bad choices—things that don't grow your money, your time, or your peace. That's not investing; that's spending dressed up as wisdom.

Here's my line in the sand: Investment is growing your wealth by spending on the right things. Take a high-end gaming laptop—unless it's earning you cash beyond your day job, it's a toy, not an investment. Now, buying a blue-chip stock when the market's a bloodbath? That's money well spent—it grows as the chaos fades. The difference is stark: one's a burden, the other's a bridge. We kneel under the first and rise with the second.

***

The system doesn't want you to see that. Banks thrive when you borrow, not when you build. Governments tweak policies to keep the machine humming, and we're the fuel—our wallets, our debts. A raise lands in your account, and what's the reflex? Not to save more, not to invest more—to owe more. A bigger house, a flashier car, a phone on EMI. Society nods, "You've earned it." Your ego chimes in, “Show it.” But every debt is a chain. You’re not climbing; you’re sinking.

I’ve felt that pull. When I started at the bank in 2007—my first job—I had no offers, no savings, no account. Just a degree and a paycheck. Three months in, I quit—no backup job, just a gut feeling it wasn’t for me. But I left with something: a bank account and a little cash. That was my first step—not much, but a start. Then came the startup in July 2007. Everything was fresh—new city, new risks. I started saving, tiny amounts at first, dipping my toes into investing. Small stocks, small bets. When I left in 2010, I had three offers in hand. I picked the fattest paycheck—an Indian MNC—and my salary jumped. So did my savings.

***

That move taught me something: opportunity isn’t static. I didn’t hesitate to shift cities—twice—for client projects. The company tossed in deputation allowances, and my income climbed again. By 2011, I’d landed at my first international MNC. Two offers on the table, and I chose the one with onshore potential. The salary spiked, and I funneled the extra into savings. July 2011, I bought my bike—not on credit, but cash (Chapter 7). Practical, not flashy. It saved me hours, not pride. When I moved to the US in 2015, the game changed—dollars, not rupees. My savings ballooned when I converted them back home. I kept it simple: no car loans, no house debt—just cash for what I needed (Chapter 8).

Back in India by 2021, I joined my second Indian MNC. Two offers again, and I took the higher one. Along the way, my savings grew—not just in the bank, but in stocks, gold, term insurance. Debt? Not really. I've dodged it like a plague. Each raise didn't bloat my lifestyle—it built my reserves. What's the payoff? Peace of mind. A good night's sleep. What more can you ask for?

***

This is my quirk: I chase the salary, not the debt. Every job switch, every move, was a grab for more income—not to spend, but to stack. When I started at the bank, I had nothing. When I left, I had a foothold. The startup stretched me thin, but I saved anyway. Each MNC jump—Indian, international, back to Indian—pushed my earnings up, and I let my savings ride the wave. No loans, no EMIs. Just cash and choices. I didn't play to the gallery, piling on burdens to look the part. I chose my own way—more money in, more money kept.

Ayn Rand said, "Wealth is the product of man's capacity to think." She's right. Your salary's your tool—use it to think, not to kneel. I could've financed a car in the US—plenty did—but I saved and bought it outright. I could've grabbed a bigger house with a loan in 2021, but I waited, built it debt-free (Chapter 8). My raises didn't buy me status; they bought me freedom. Contrast that with a friend at the startup—he took a loan for a wedding, and five years later, he's still paying it off. Same starting point, different paths.

***

Here's the shift: Increase your salary, not your debts. It's not about how much you make—it's about how much you keep, how much you grow. Every extra buck should fuel your ascent—bank accounts, stocks, skills—not chain you to repayments. The system wants you laden; it profits when you're a camel. But you don't have to kneel. You're a builder.

Nietzsche said, "Hitherto, there have been more followers than leaders." Most kneel—loans for cars, EMIs for phones, debts to impress. I've moved cities, switched jobs, chased dollars, all to stack my chips—not to show off, but to sleep easy. What about you? The next time you get a raise, ask yourself—will this buy me freedom, or another chain? Will you bend under burdens you don't need, playing to the gallery? Or will you write your own way—salary up, debts down, freedom yours?

***

Interlude

We've journeyed through ten chapters of the philosophical journey, "**Unwritten: Write Your Fate**", each rooted in my experiences. Before we move forward, I want to pause and clarify a few things. This isn't about preaching—it's about sharing what I've learned, hoping it sparks reflection in you.

Let's start with my examples, like mortgages, car loans, personal loans, and phone EMIs. They're often drawn from the Indian context, reflecting what I've seen around me. You might notice I lean on these frequently, and that's intentional. They're the financial traps I've observed most, the ones that ensnare people I know. My perspective shapes this book, and these examples fit the lessons I'm sharing. As we progress, I'll weave in new contexts where the topics call for it, ensuring the examples evolve naturally with the narrative.

This book is my lens, my learning—no more, no less. Ayn Rand said, "The truth is not for all men, but only for those who seek it." I'm not here to dictate your truth, just to offer mine, seeking clarity through my own financial choices. The philosophies I've drawn on—Nietzsche's rejection of herd mentality, Rand's focus on rational self-interest, Socrates' call for self-knowledge—aren't just abstract ideas. They're deeply interlinked with financial matters, guiding how I approach money. Nietzsche taught me to question society's spending scripts; Rand showed me money as a tool for rational control; Socrates urged me to know my financial self. These ideas aren't separate from finance—they're its foundation.

I've shared my story not to boast, but to show what's possible. This journey is about writing your own fate, not following the herd. Most people conform, borrowing to belong, spending to impress. I've tried to walk my own path, seeking my truth through deliberate choices. So, take a moment: Are you choosing your financial path with intention, or drifting with the crowd? What does your money say about your truth?

***

Chapter 11 - Budgeting and Tracking Expenses

"The unexamined life is not worth living," Socrates famously declared. That profound truth extends to our finances. Not knowing what's coming up for the next month in terms of expenses is an ignorant place to be. But can we predict the unknown? Can we see the future? If so, we'd be called seers or people with a hyper-accurate sixth sense. The problem is—we're not. We are, however, responsible for examining the financial aspects of our lives that are within our control.

And yet, there's a middle ground. We may not foresee the unpredictable, but we can absolutely plan for what's within our control. We should know, at the very least, the recurring and expected expenses for the upcoming weeks.

How often have you moved through a month without planning your expenses? It's like working for a company without knowing what they'll pay you. Would you do that? Would you put in hours, pour in effort, and take risks without ensuring compensation? No. You'd demand clarity. Yet, when it comes to our own spending, we move blindly, with no structure or oversight.

Why? Because we tell ourselves money is meant to be spent. We work for it, we earn it, so what's the big deal if we use it freely? That mindset is the root of financial indiscipline. It's why so many people live paycheck to paycheck, why unexpected expenses derail financial stability, why months go by where expenses outstrip income. And that's a financial abyss.

***

Financial control starts with two fundamental habits: budgeting and tracking expenses. Budgeting is the preemptive strike—you define how much goes where *before* you spend a dime. It accounts for fixed expenses (rent, utilities, insurance), variable expenses (groceries, dining out, transportation), and unknown expenses (unexpected repairs, medical emergencies, impulse decisions). Without budgeting, you're walking into a storm blindfolded, reacting instead of acting.

Tracking expenses, on the other hand, is the reality check. Budgeting lays out the plan; tracking tells you how well you're sticking to it. It exposes leaks, indulgences, and financial drift. Many people assume they know where their money is going—until they track every penny and realize how much is wasted.

Here's my personal system: I've maintained a budgeting spreadsheet for years. Every month, I list my income—salary, interest earnings, dividends, any side income. Then, I break down expected expenses, allocating a small buffer of 1.5k rupees for miscellaneous expenses. And when I overspend the budget, the first thing I do with the next paycheck is to refill the same amount to my salary account to match the balance to the one that I got right after my previous month's budget. This approach helps me stay disciplined. What's left is my investment capital. This isn't just a record-keeping exercise; it's a strategy.

Though my financial philosophy has evolved, my budgeting principles remain unchanged. When I was at a startup, I didn't budget formally, but I practiced an indirect form of it—setting aside half my salary in an untouched account. During my days in my first Indian multinational, I did the same. With high-interest rates back then, parking cash in savings accounts felt like investing. At my days in international MNC, the method continued.

Then I moved to the US, and things changed. My spouse introduced a structured monthly budgeting system, ensuring our expenses were in check. Even today, I stick to a strict principle: my savings and investments must never fall below 40% of my take-home salary. The moment my budget is finalized, I transfer the surplus into my investment accounts immediately—before I have the chance to spend it elsewhere. No temptation, no second-guessing. A forced discipline that ensures long-term financial growth.

If you have a partner who doesn't align with this philosophy, it's tough. Financial discipline thrives on alignment; if one person budgets and the other splurges, tension is inevitable. Money habits, like any aspect of a relationship, require mutual understanding.

***

Budgeting is one side of the coin. Tracking expenses is the other. Budgeting tells you what should happen. Tracking tells you what actually happened. If you don't track, you won't know when your money deviates from your plan. You'll spend money set aside for investments on impulsive purchases. You'll convince yourself it's "just this once," only to realize you've done it three times in a week. Tracking is where financial awareness becomes financial control.

I learned expense tracking from my father. As a child, I watched him meticulously document every single expenditure in a diary. He'd go through his notes, reconciling where money went, ensuring nothing slipped through the cracks. By the time I hit the 5th grade, the habit was ingrained in me. Since 2011, I've tracked every single rupee I've spent, and I still do it today. Old habits die hard.

Today, I use a mobile app for real-time tracking. Every purchase, every bill, every transaction—I log it. Some argue that modern banks already categorize expenses, so why bother tracking manually? Because convenience kills accountability.

Think about it—how often do you actually check your bank's expense tracker? Rarely. You know it's there, you assume it's accurate, and you move on. That's passive tracking, not active awareness. When you manually track your expenses, you're constantly conscious of where your money is going. It forces accountability.

***

"Know thyself," Socrates said, a vital financial truth. Lack of spending awareness, not income, causes most money problems. Can you recall last month's spending details? If not, money controls you. Financial mastery relies on budgeting and expense tracking. Budgeting assigns each rupee a role before spending. Tracking reveals actual spending. Neglecting either invites chaos. A budget without tracking is self-deception; tracking without budgeting, regret.

Budgeting dictates *what should happen*; tracking, *what did.* Without tracking, impulsive spending erodes plans. Manual tracking, unlike bank categorization, fosters awareness. My father instilled this habit. Convenience undermines accountability.

"Know thyself" applies to finance. Know your income, expenses, and patterns. A simple test: can you recall last month's spending? If not, money controls you.

The process: budget before spending, track every rupee spent. Missing either step collapses the system. The financially stable control more, they don't necessarily earn more. Budgeting and tracking are tools, not chores. Master them, and you master money. Ignore them, and money masters you. The world encourages reactive spending. If you don't budget and track, money controls you. Where is your money going?

***

Chapter 12 - Bad Debt and Bad Investment

How do we define what's good or bad in a world obsessed with judging us by its own virtues? Society doesn't just label us—it pressures us to conform. If we don't, we're branded rebels, outcasts, or worse, people with "no virtues." But who decides how we should act? Should we take the bait and bend to these expectations? Religion, morality, social norms—they're all cut from the same cloth, designed to maintain order, control the masses, and build a "healthy" society. Yet, in that design, they often pull down the weak, the individual, in ways so subtle we barely notice. They're meant to make society progress, not collapse, but they can collapse us in the process.

Think about it: How many times have you given in to societal pressure? Is society funding your life to dictate how you spend your money? Most of our choices aren't truly ours—they're shaped by the world around us. If you pause and reflect on the decisions you've made under this pressure, you'll see some were bad, even reluctant. Some became financial burdens, weights you'll carry for years. Who benefits? Society does—it gets its show, its order. But when the consequences hit, does society take responsibility? No. You're left holding the bag, paying the price for choices you didn't fully own.

***

Ayn Rand cut through the noise: "Anything that is detrimental to rational self-interest is bad." It's that simple, and it's a lens we can use to spot bad debt and bad investments. Mental conditioning is everything in finance. We live in a society, but not for it. The day you realize this, you're free from the herd. Nietzsche would call this liberation—stepping out of the follower's role to become your own shepherd. When you rule yourself, societal pressure loses its grip, and you become more money-conscious, more deliberate. But how do we define bad debt or a bad investment? Here's my take: If you break your bank for society's sake, it's bad debt. If you sink money into something that doesn't grow your wealth or peace, it's a bad investment.

Let's start with bad debt. Consider the societal ritual of marriage in India. Tradition demands a grand wedding—inviting everyone: uncles, aunts, cousins, grandparents, neighbors, friends from school, college, work. Back in the day, this made sense with joint families, where everyone was intertwined. But now, with nuclear families on the rise, does it? The common logic is "getting blessings from all," a sentiment tied to feeding people during life events. But let's be real—how many come to bless you, and how many come for the feast? No offense, just my interpretation. I've seen people take personal loans at high interest rates for a lavish wedding. For what? A memory? Two days of enjoyment? A show of status? Even without loans, many drain their savings to get married. It's a spectacle, not a union. To me, marriage is a personal commitment, a legal bond between two people. Why the exaggeration?

When I got married, I kept it simple. I bought five pairs of jeans, five shirts and t-shirts, and a suit—the simplest, cheapest options I could find. That was it. Looking back, I regret not contributing more to the expenses, as tradition often burdens the bridegroom's family. If two people are marrying, shouldn't the costs be shared? I wish I'd pushed for that, but it was my first time getting married—what did I know? Joking aside, I know the financial strain fell on my spouse's side, and I regret that. My father handled other costs, though I'm not sure of the details. For the reception, we booked a modest party hall, hosting just 20 colleagues and five school friends. No extravagance, just enough. That choice saved us from the bad debt of a wedding we couldn't afford, but I still wish I'd done more to balance the load.

***

Once married, the next societal pressure hits: buy a house. I faced this head-on. I was in the US for three months before returning to India for my wedding in 2015, then heading back to the US a couple of weeks later. During that time, my spouse urged me multiple times to buy a house in India. The logic? We'd get rental yield. My counter? We don't live in it, we don't have the cash to buy outright, we'd need a mortgage, and we'd be paying for something we don't own until the last EMI. The rental income wouldn't cover the EMI—it didn't add up. I resisted that pressure until I had enough to buy a house without a loan. Now we live in it, debt-free, with no rent to pay. It's peace of mind. Had I bought it while in the US, it would've been a bad investment—a drain, not a gain.

Society doesn't stop there. After a house, it's a car. I've delayed buying one in India, even now. Cars depreciate the moment you drive them off the lot. A rarely used car is a bad investment—money tied up in a wasting asset. A used car makes more sense, but society pushes for new, shiny, status-driven purchases. I'd rather spend that money on something that grows me—like learning a new technology or getting certified in my field. Gadgets are another trap. A 55-inch TV to decorate your living room? That's a bad investment—it just sits there, unused, while its value drops. Compare that to investing in solar panels or energy solutions, which I've considered seriously. They'd give me long-term benefits—lower electricity bills, sustainable savings, maybe even surplus energy to sell back to the grid. That's a real return, unlike something that lies unused, gathering dust. I'd rather invest in knowledge, something that pays dividends in opportunity.

***

Socrates summed it up: "Good is knowledge, and bad is ignorance." Only when you know what's happening around you can you discern what's good. Ignorance of your actions leads to financial drain—it's inevitable. When I was in the US, I could've caved to the house pressure, taking a mortgage, I couldn't justify. But I knew the numbers didn't work, and that knowledge saved me. My wedding could've been a financial disaster, but awareness kept it modest. Each choice was a rejection of ignorance, a step toward good.

Nietzsche's perspectivism fits here: there are no facts, only interpretations. A house isn't inherently a good investment—it depends on your lens. For me, a house I couldn't live in, bought with debt, was a bad interpretation of wealth. A car I wouldn't use? Same. Society interprets these as markers of success; I see them as burdens. Rand's Objectivism doubles down: if it doesn't serve your rational self-interest, it's bad. A wedding loan for show doesn't serve you—it serves the herd. A depreciating car doesn't build your future—it builds someone else's image of you.

***

The herd wants you to conform. But conformity comes at a cost. I've seen people take wedding loans, still paying them off years later. Others bought houses they couldn't afford, trapped by EMIs, unable to save. Cars sit unused, gadgets gather dust, all for the sake of "looking successful." Who's winning here? Not them. The banks, the retailers, the society that claps for the show—they win. You lose.

I've tried to walk a different path. My wedding wasn't a spectacle—it was a commitment. My house wasn't a status symbol—it was a home, bought when I could afford it, debt-free. I don't own a car, and I don't miss it. These choices weren't easy—pressure is real, and regret stings. I still wish I'd shared more of my wedding costs, easing the strain on my spouse's family. But each decision was mine, not society's, and that's the point. Nietzsche would say I'm rejecting the herd; Rand would say I'm serving my rational self-interest. Socrates would say I'm choosing knowledge over ignorance.

Bad debt and bad investments aren't just financial mistakes—they're choices to let society write your story. Know why you're spending, know what it costs, know what it builds. If it doesn't serve your future, your peace, your growth, it's bad—period. I've made my choices, some with regret, some with pride. I've shared them not to judge, but to show what's possible when you question the script. So, what's your next financial move? Will you borrow for the herd, invest for the show? Or will you choose knowledge, writing a story that's yours, not theirs?

***

Chapter 13 - The XYZ Rule

We often find ourselves gazing at successful people, hoping to draw inspiration from their achievements. Their stories captivate us—tales of wealth, fame, and financial mastery. We're quick to adopt their strategies, convinced that their methods will lead us to the same heights. But why are we so eager to follow their paths? Why do we assume their rules will work for us? The answer lies in a simple, human desire: we crave the easiest route to success. We'd rather leap toward victory than trudge through the hard work of carving our own way. Nietzsche warned us about this trap: "Convictions are more dangerous enemies of truth than lies." In our rush to emulate others, we often abandon critical thinking, placing blind trust in someone else's blueprint. It's a perilous journey. You might reach a destination, but is it yours? By the time you realize it's not, you've lost precious time and effort chasing someone else's dream.

Consider the era before the internet. Did the successful figures of that time have role models to copy? Some did, but many didn't. They had to discover what worked for them through trial and error, often failing multiple times before striking gold. Did they build wealth on their first try? Rarely. So why do we assume that mimicking a modern success story will guarantee our own? It's because we're conditioned to seek instant results. We want the shortcut, the magic formula. But in that pursuit, we overlook a vital skill: the ability to analyze, to question, to think for ourselves. Blindly following someone else's path is like driving with your eyes closed—you might move forward, but you'll likely crash.

***

You've probably come across financial "rules" on platforms like YouTube—formulas promising to secure your future. Take the XYZ rule, for instance, often framed as something like 20-15-30: when buying a house, have 20% as a down payment, keep the loan tenure under 15 years, and ensure the EMI is less than 30% of your monthly income. These rules are designed to guide financial planning, offering a structured approach to big decisions. They sound reasonable, even wise, and for many, they might work. But should they be taken as gospel? I don't think so. To me, they're guidelines, not commandments. There's no universal law etched in stone that guarantees success for everyone.

Let's break this down. Imagine someone who can buy a house outright—do they need to worry about a 20% down payment or loan tenure? Of course not. Now consider someone who can't repay a mortgage in 15 years. They might opt for a longer tenure to manage cash flow, even if it deviates from the rule. Or take someone eager to clear their mortgage quickly—they might ignore the EMI cap, choosing a higher payment to be debt-free sooner. The permutations are endless. A rule that fits one person's life might be a mismatch for another's. That's why introspection is key. You have to weigh these guidelines against your own circumstances, goals, and instincts.

What works for a billionaire on YouTube might not work for you, and that's okay.

***

So, how did I navigate my financial path? I've mentioned before, in the chapter on action planning, that I don't follow any single person or rule. Instead, I listen to many voices, picking up fragments that resonate with my way of thinking. It's a bit like philosophy—you don't have to commit to one thinker or school of thought. Each philosopher offers unique perspectives that spark curiosity. I find value in Nietzsche's skepticism of herd mentality, Rand's emphasis on rational self-interest, and Socrates' call for self-knowledge. I take what speaks to me, blend it with my own understanding, and create something that fits my life. That's how I've approached money, too.

I've never been one for rigid formulas. My strategy has been straightforward: save before I spend, and invest a significant portion of my income—often more than 50% of my salary each month. It wasn't always perfect. I'm not perfect now, and I never will be. I've missed golden opportunities to invest, like not jumping into the market early enough. I started my investment journey later than I should have, and that cost me. But I've learned from those mistakes. The past isn't there to haunt you—it's there to teach you. I can't waste time dwelling on what might have been if I'd chosen differently. Instead, I focus on covering lost ground, building on what I've learned, and moving forward.

***

Ayn Rand once said, "Integrity is the ability to stand by an idea." That's the crux of it: how much do you trust your own instincts? How strongly do you believe in the financial approach you've tailored for yourself? Confidence in your own ideas, even if they differ from the crowd, is what drives success. It might seem stubborn, even rude, to stick to your ground when everyone else is following a popular rule. But in the end, you're the one who benefits. No one else loses when you prioritize your journey over society's expectations. Your path, your rules.

For me, this meant rejecting the XYZ rule—or any rule—when it didn't fit my reality. I didn't buy a house when societal pressure demanded it, as I shared in the last chapter. I saved aggressively, invested heavily, and learned from my missteps. I didn't depend on a YouTube guru's formula to tell me how to manage my money. I figured out what worked for me through experience, reflection, and a willingness to adapt. That's not to say I ignored advice—I listened, but I filtered it through my own lens. What aligned with my goals, I kept. What didn't, I discarded.

***

The XYZ rule, or any financial formula, can be a starting point, but it's not the finish line. Success comes from understanding your own needs, strengths, and weaknesses. Take the house-buying example again. If you're someone who values mobility, maybe renting makes more sense than buying, regardless of what the rule says. Or if you're saving for another goal—like starting a business—you might delay buying altogether. The key is to think critically, not blindly.

This applies to investing, too. I've always prioritized investments that grow my future, like education or skills, over flashy purchases that depreciate. But I've also made mistakes—missing early investment opportunities taught me the value of timing. I didn't let those mistakes define me. Instead, I adjusted, learned, and kept going. That's what I mean by crafting your own path. You can hear the success stories, study the rules, but in the end, you have to implement what suits you. It's about standing by your own ideas, even when they don't match the crowd's.

***

Blind trust in someone else's strategy is a dangerous game. I've tried to avoid that trap. My financial journey—from starting with nothing in 2007 to building savings and investments now—has been about questioning, learning, and adapting. I didn't follow blindly. Learned from my mistakes. I stood by my own ideas, even when they went against the grain. That's what's brought me peace of mind—not a borrowed formula, but a path I carved myself.

In the end, create your own rule. Trust your instincts, even if they lead you away from the crowd. It's your journey, your ideas, your fate. I've shared my path not to say it's the only way, but to show what's possible when you think for yourself. I've made mistakes, learned lessons, and kept going. What about you? What will you choose: a borrowed dream or a destiny of your own making?

***

Chapter 14: The Power to Command Yourself

"He who cannot obey himself will be commanded," Nietzsche once said. I read that line in my early twenties, back when I was just starting out at the bank in 2007, barely getting started with my career. It didn't hit me fully then—I was too busy waiting for my paycheck to arrive, dreaming of the things I'd buy. But over the years, as I navigated job switches, moved to the US, and built a life free of debt, those words started to sink in. If I couldn't control my own impulses, someone—or something—else would. In the realm of money, that "something" is the world itself, with its endless temptations to spend, borrow, and conform. This chapter is about taking command of yourself, your resources, and your fate. It's about ensuring that what you earn remains yours to use, not to lose.

What we earn is ours. It sounds simple, doesn't it? But here's the catch: it's only ours until we have it for our use. Once it's gone, it's gone forever. There's no magical refund policy for a life spent chasing fleeting pleasures. For most of us, this is a lesson learned the hard way—waiting for that paycheck to arrive, only to spend it on things we think we need, like an extra pair of shoes that barely gets worn or a shiny new gadget that loses its charm in a month. It wasn't until I started flipping the script—saving first, spending later—that I realized what it meant to truly own my earnings. As I've shared in earlier chapters, my routine became ironclad: repay debt first to my friend, save aggressively, and then spend what's left. Debt repayment was always the priority—getting rid of those shackles meant I could breathe easier. Once that was done, I'd save, and only then would I spend. But here's the thing: I don't spend on just anything.

Do I splurge on unwanted things? Not really. But what even counts as "unwanted"? That's where things get tricky—it's subjective. Everyone's got their own objectives, their own version of what makes a purchase "worth it." For me, eating out is money well spent. I love a good meal—it's a small joy that keeps me grounded, a reward after a long week of sticking to my budget. But for someone else, buying the latest gadget might be their idea of money well spent. Another person might feel alive watching a movie in a theater, munching on popcorn with a Coke in hand. Who am I to judge? We're all different, with different needs and desires. The key, though, is what you do before you even think about spending: you save. That's the rule of thumb I've lived by since 2011, when I started getting serious about my finances. Save first, then decide what "well spent" means to you.

***

Saving and investing—they're two sides of the same coin. You can interchange them based on your preferences, but ultimately, investing is a form of saving too. It's about securing your money for a better, more confident future. Some folks might push back on this. I've heard the argument plenty of times: "We don't even know what tomorrow holds. What if I die in an accident? Why bother saving if I might not be around to enjoy it?" It's a fair point. Life's uncertain—we could get sick and die tomorrow. But let's flip that around. What are the odds of that actually happening? Now, what if you don't get sick? What if you survive the odds and live to 70, 80, or even 90? Would you rather regret the decisions you made not to save, or would you rather enjoy the benefits of your past choices? I'd choose the latter every time. That's what I call prepping for the worst. Living to 70 isn't some distant dream—it's the worst-case scenario I plan for. If I'm wrong and I don't make it that far, well, at least I lived with intention. But if I'm right, I'll be ready.

***

If you don't have money, the world isn't a kind place to survive. You'll be commanded—by bills, by debt, by the expectations of a society that wants you to keep spending. Is there a way out? Not without money, there isn't. That's where self-control and discipline come in. Nietzsche's words keep echoing in my mind: obey yourself, or someone else will. For me, that self-obedience looks like a habit I've cultivated over years—saving and investing first, spending second. Once that routine became second nature, breaking it felt unthinkable. It's like brushing your teeth—you don't debate whether to do it; you just do. Building that habit isn't easy, especially in a world designed to tempt you at every turn. But once it's there, it's your shield against being commanded by anyone or anything else.

Money is power. It's the power to survive the odds, the power to live on your terms, and the power to be proud of the life you've built. Plato once said, "The measure of a man is what he does with power." In our capitalist world, money is the driving force behind that power. It's what lets you achieve what you desire—whether that's a debt-free home, like the one I bought in 2024, or the freedom to walk away from a job you hate. Waiting for paychecks to arrive won't make you rich, but working with your money will. I'm not talking about slaving away at a desk—I mean making your money work for you. It should be growing, even when you're sleeping. That's where investing comes in. It's not just about saving for the future; it's about building a future where you're not at the mercy of the next bill.

***

So, what's the right amount to save or invest each month? That's subjective too—everyone's got their own goals. But if you want to live frugally, I'd say at least 60% of your income should go toward saving or investing. That's what I've followed for years, and I plan to keep it up. It's a step up from the 50% I started with back in 2011, a tweak I made as my income grew and my discipline sharpened. That 60% rule forces you to rethink your lifestyle—it fine-tunes your mind to live lean, to prioritize what matters. Why frugal living? Because the capitalist world is a trap. It's designed to lure you into spending on things you don't need. Think about it: how many times have you bought something on a whim, only to let it gather dust? Look around your house—how many unused items are sitting there, mocking you? That's where your money's been going all these years. I used to fall into that trap too, back in my early days, buying gadgets I thought would make me happy. They didn't. What made me happy was the security of knowing I could handle whatever life threw at me.

At the end of the day, think about you and only you. There's a saying I've always loved: "Even your shadow leaves you when it's dark." No one's coming to rescue you in this chaotic world—not your friends, not your family, not the system. The only one you can truly rely on is yourself. That's why I save, why I invest, why I live frugally. It's not about deprivation—it's about empowerment. It's about obeying myself so I'm never commanded by anyone else. Nietzsche knew what he was talking about, and I've spent the last 18 years proving it, one paycheck at a time. So, consider this approach: save first, invest wisely, and spend on what truly matters to you. That's how you write your fate.

***

Chapter 15: Inflation

"You can ignore reality, but you can't ignore the consequences of ignoring reality," Ayn Rand once wrote. I didn't fully grasp that truth until inflation slapped me in the face. For the longest time—well into my early thirties—I thought inflation was just a fancy word for price rises. It was something I heard about on the news or in passing conversations, but I never stopped to think about what it actually meant for me. I was too busy building my life, moving to the US by 2015, then back to India in 2021, all while sticking to my principles of saving first and spending wisely. But when I returned to India after six years abroad, reality hit hard. Inflation isn't just a price rise—it's a silent killer, a cancer you can't cure, and its everywhere money is involved. This chapter is about facing that reality head-on, understanding its consequences, and learning how to fight back with purpose.

I'll never forget the moment inflation became real to me. It was 2021, shortly after I'd come back to India from the US. I walked into a familiar grocery store, the kind I'd been shopping at since 2010 to early days in 2015, before I left for the US. I picked up a few staples—some rice, lentils, a couple of vegetables—thinking I knew exactly what the bill would be. I'd done these routine countless times before. But when I got to the counter, the total was at least 50% more than what I'd paid for the same items six years ago. I stood there, stunned, as the cashier handed me the receipt. I hadn't bought more; the prices had just skyrocketed. From that day on, I started paying closer attention. I'd pick up an item, flip it over, and check the price on the back, mentally comparing it to what I'd paid in 2015. A kilogram of rice that cost 50 rupees back then was now 75. A liter of oil that was 80 rupees was now 160. Let that sink in. That's inflation—and it's a harsh teacher.

***

In India, inflation usually hovers around 6-7% a year. That might not sound like much, but it adds up. Most of the time, you won't see it in the headlines—it's just a quiet, steady creep. But when it spikes to 8-10%, that's when it makes news. The central bank steps in, raising interest rates to cool things down, and suddenly everyone's talking about it. But here's the hard reality: prices don't go back down when inflation eases. If an item costs 10 rupees at 6% inflation, it might jump to 12 rupees when inflation hits 9%. But even if inflation drops back to 6%, that item isn't going back to 10 rupees. It'll stay at 12, or maybe drop to 11 if you're lucky. That's what economists call price stickiness, and it's a one-way street. The only exceptions are rare, unlabeled items—like vegetables or snacks from street vendors—where prices might fluctuate more directly with inflation. But for most things, the new price is the new normal. That grocery bill in 2021 wasn't a fluke; it was a wake-up call.

If we ignore this fact—that inflation eats away at our money—we're setting ourselves up for failure. Rand was right: you can pretend inflation doesn't exist, but you can't escape the consequences. Unfortunately, most of us don't fight the weed at its roots—we just deal with the fallout. We grumble about higher prices, adjust our budgets, and move on, never addressing the core issue. I've seen it happen all around me. People who used to buy five burgers for a weekend treat now settle for two, not because they're eating less, but because that's all their money can buy. The same amount of cash that got you a full meal a few years ago now barely covers a snack. That's inflation at work, eroding your purchasing power while you're not looking. If you're not careful, it'll leave you with nothing but regrets.

Let's do the math to see how insidious this is. Say you save your hard-earned money in a bank account that gives you 3% annual interest. Sounds like a safe bet, right? Now, let's say inflation is running at 6%—pretty standard in India. That means you're losing 3% of your money's value every year. The term "saving" is deceptively attractive. We all think that by putting money in a savings account and leaving it untouched for a few years, we're securing our future—maybe for a house, a car, or a rainy day. But the reality is starkly different. That 3% loss compounds over time. In 10 years, your money's purchasing power could be cut by nearly a third. You'll still have the same amount in your account, sure, but what it can buy will be far less. A 1000-rupee bill that could fill a grocery cart in 2015 might barely cover half the cart by 2025. That's the consequence of ignoring reality, and it's a lesson I refused to learn the hard way.

This is where purpose comes into the picture, as Rand so powerfully pointed out: "The most depraved type of human being ... is the man without a purpose." Saving with the wrong instrument is like locking your valuables in a box that's slowly leaking through the cracks. The intention to save is right, but the approach matters just as much. If you're serious about protecting your money, you need to invest in instruments that at least match inflation, if not beat it. Stocks, bonds, gold, even real estate in some cases—these can offer returns that keep your money's purchasing power intact or even grow it. I learned this lesson over time, and it's shaped how I handle my savings to this day.

***

Back in the early 2010s, I used to park my savings in a bank account that gave me a decent 9% annual interest. It felt like a win—my money was growing, and I wasn't touching it. But by the time I returned to India in 2021, things had changed. That same bank was now offering just 3.5% interest, while inflation was still running at 6-7%. I did the math and realized I was losing money every year, even though my account balance was going up. It was a bitter pill to swallow. So, I took action. I moved my savings into instruments that gave me higher returns. I wasn't chasing risky get-rich-quick schemes; I just wanted to beat inflation and protect what I'd worked so hard to earn. At the end of the day, who wants to lose money to thin air? Inflation is a parasite, and you have to be aware of it to act accordingly.

***

This ties back to everything I've been building since 2007. As I've shared in earlier chapters, my journey has been about rejecting the traps society sets for us—whether it's the wedding loans I avoided in my twenties, the XYZ rules I dismissed in Chapter 13, or the consumerist pressure to spend more as prices rise. Inflation is another one of those traps, but it's sneakier. It doesn't announce itself with a big warning sign; it just chips away at your resources until you're left wondering where it all went. The establishment doesn't want you to notice. They'd rather you keep spending, keep borrowing, keep playing their game. But I've never been one to follow the herd. As Nietzsche reminded us in Chapter 14, if you can't obey yourself, you'll be commanded. For me, that self-obedience means staying vigilant, even against silent killers like inflation.

So, what's the way forward? First, don't just save—invest with purpose. Look for options that at least match inflation, if not beat it. If you're earning 3% while inflation is at 6%, you're not saving—you're losing. Second, live frugally, as I've always done. When prices started climbing in 2021, I didn't start spending more to "keep up." I doubled down on my habits—cooking at home more, saving aggressively (60% of my income, as I mentioned in Chapter 14), and spending only on what truly matters, like the occasional meal out that brings me joy. Third, stay aware. Inflation isn't a one-time event; it's a constant force. Keep an eye on prices, adjust your strategy as needed, and never stop learning about how to protect your money.

Inflation is a reality we can't ignore, but we can control how we respond to it. I've spent the last 18 years writing my own fate, from my early days in India to my time in the US and back again. Through it all, I've faced inflation's challenges by staying purposeful—rejecting passive saving, embracing smart investing, and living on my terms. As you navigate your own journey, consider this approach: don't let inflation erode your hard-earned money. Face the reality, beat the parasite, and write your fate with intention.

***

Chapter 16: Insurance and Emergency Funds

It's easy to assume nothing will go wrong. We wake up each day, go through our routines, and tell ourselves that the worst won't happen—at least not to us. But the reality is starkly different. Something is bound to happen; it's a ticking time bomb waiting to go off. No one can predict the future—not the greatest prophets, not even the sharpest minds. Prophecies are a scam, a distraction from the truth we'd rather ignore. At best, we might know what's coming in the next hour. Maybe the next eight hours, if we're lucky. But beyond that? We're all busy anticipating the best, conveniently brushing the worst under the rug. That's the elephant in the room, and it's been there all along, waiting for us to acknowledge it.

Ayn Rand put it perfectly: "Man survives by the guidance of his mind. If his basic premises are wrong, his life is doomed." I've carried that idea with me through every step of my journey. It's a principle I've touched on before, back in Chapter 14 when I talked about commanding yourself to avoid being commanded by the world. The basic premise I'm speaking of is simple: prepare for the worst. That's the foundation that should guide your mind, your actions, your entire approach to life. Imagine getting hospitalized and watching your savings vanish to cover the bill. Imagine the breadwinner of a family no longer being there to keep things running. Or picture an unexpected expense—something unavoidable—popping up out of nowhere. These aren't just hypotheticals; they're the guiding principles that should shape every decision you make. When your motives align with this mindset, your nights become peaceful, and your days become productive. It's not just about survival—it's a kind of motivation to build a better present and a secure future.

There are a few key aspects to this preparation, a few things we need to protect to ensure we're not caught off guard. I break them down into four areas: health, stability, house, and future. Each one requires its own shield, a way to safeguard what you've built without letting the world's uncertainties dictate your path. Let's dive into each, drawing from my own journey and the lessons I've learned along the way.

***

Protecting Your Health: Your health is your first line of defense. Medical inflation is a beast—it's running at roughly 15% a year. Can you imagine paying an exorbitant amount for a simple procedure or a couple of days in the hospital? That's the sad reality we're facing. The cost of healthcare is climbing faster than most of us can keep up with, and it's not slowing down. I saw this firsthand when I returned to India in 2021, and was operated for a minor issue. A routine doctor's visit that cost 200 rupees in 2015 was now 800, and hospital stays were even worse. The best way to protect yourself is to prioritize your health—eat well, exercise, stay mindful. But in our busy schedules, that's easier said than done. I'll admit, I've struggled with this myself, especially during my years in the US when long work hours left little time for self-care.

So, what's the next best option? Health insurance for the entire family.

A good health insurance cover should be equivalent to at least two years of your household spending. That's the minimum I'd recommend to feel secure. But here's where I'll be honest: I haven't taken out my own health insurance policy yet. Right now, I rely on my employer's cover, which comes with its own risks. It's a tricky situation. If I resign and move to another company, I'll be without coverage from the day I exit until the new employer's policy kicks in. Who knows what could happen in those few days? It's a dependency I'm not comfortable with, and I've realized I need to act. I'm working on getting my own personal health insurance by the end of 2025, but in the meantime, I've taken steps to mitigate the risk. I've added an add-on cover that's three times the amount of my employer's base cover, a life cover that's twice what the employer provides, the maximum accidental death cover I could choose, and comprehensive coverage for most diseases. On top of that, I've insured my parents with a top-up plan as well. It's not perfect, but it's the best I can do until I have my own policy in place. This interim setup gives me some peace of mind, but I know I need to take full control soon.

***

Protecting Your Stability: No matter how careful you are, unexpected expenses—big or small—are inevitable. If it's a big expense, the impact on your finances can be devastating. Think about the possibilities: a sudden car repair, a family emergency, or, worst of all, the breadwinner losing their job. What does the future look like in that scenario? The bills don't wait for you to find another job. The world keeps moving, with or without you, and if you're not prepared, it'll crush you under its weight. That's where emergency funds come in—a lifeline to keep you afloat when the unexpected strikes.

The mindset here is key. You have to prepare for the unknown. You can't rely on running to friends or family for help in a crisis. I've seen too many people fall into that trap, borrowing money they can't repay and digging themselves into a deeper hole. An emergency fund gives you independence, a way to handle life's curveballs without losing your footing. But where should you park this money? It needs to be in an instrument you can liquidate immediately. Real estate, for example, is the worst place for an emergency fund. Imagine trying to sell a property when you need cash right away—it's a nightmare. Instead, opt for something accessible like fixed deposits or debt mutual funds. These are safer options that let you access your money quickly without losing value.

"You might be wondering: how much is enough?" I'd say at least 24 times your monthly expenses. That's what I've built for myself, and it's enough to sustain me for 24 months if things go south. Knowing I have that buffer lets me sleep soundly at night. Is that a thumb rule? Absolutely not. There are no hard rules in this world—something I've been saying. But if you're starting from scratch, aim for at least six months' worth of expenses as a baseline. That's the bare minimum to give you some breathing room. If you haven't started building your emergency fund yet, don't wait—start today. Every time you're tempted to eat out, redirect that money to your emergency fund instead. Or take 5% of your salary each month and park it the moment you get paid. Gradually increase that percentage over time. Any spending you can avoid—those impulse buys you realize you don't need—put that money into your fund. There are countless ways to start filling this bucket, but the real question is: do you have the intention to begin? For me, the answer was yes. I've got my emergency fund in place, and it's one of the best decisions I've made.

***

Protecting Your House: Winston Churchill once said, "He who fails to plan is planning to fail." I couldn't agree more, especially when it comes to the unexpected events that can threaten your home. Fire, storms, earthquakes, riots—the world is full of possibilities, both positive and negative. Your home is the one place where you can truly be yourself, a sanctuary that shields you from the chaos outside. Isn't it worth protecting? Of course it is. You've poured years of sweat and effort into building your house—it's a temple, a sacred space. Insuring it isn't just a good idea; it's a no-brainer.

In many Western countries, home insurance is mandatory, but in India, it's not. That doesn't mean you should skip it. It's your conscience that should drive this decision, not a legal requirement. When I moved to my house in 2024, I knew I needed to protect it. I've done my homework on this, and I'm planning to insure it by mid-2025, when the house will be about 3.5 years old. The ideal time to insure is when the building is less than five years old—that's when you get the best deals on premiums. My plan is to estimate the value of the house, including all belongings, and then add 25-50% more to the coverage amount. Why the extra buffer? Because premiums typically stay the same for most of the tenure, but rebuilding costs can rise with inflation, as we saw in Chapter 15. I'll also choose the maximum tenure allowed and add on any extras based on my needs—things like coverage for natural disasters or theft. It's all about ensuring that my sanctuary stays safe, no matter what the world throws at it.

***

Finally, Protecting Your Future: Building a career takes years of hard work, but all that effort can unravel in a single moment. That moment shouldn't leave your family regretting the life you've built together. Securing your future is the whole reason we work so hard—it's the endgame. For me, term insurance is an essential part of that security. The loss of a loved one is traumatizing enough; the financial uncertainty that follows shouldn't add to the pain. Imagine your family without any support after you're gone. It's a thought that's hard to bear, but it's one we need to face. Term insurance—or life insurance—ensures that your loved ones have a safety net if the worst happens.

There are two main options here: term insurance, which covers you until a certain age (like 60 or 65), and life insurance, which has no upper age limit. The choice depends on your needs. I opted for term insurance, with coverage until I'm 60. I could've gone for 65, but I decided against it. No regrets there—I took the money I would've spent on higher premiums for those extra five years and parked it in instruments that give me more than 12% returns. It's a calculated move, one that aligns with my approach to beating inflation, as I discussed in Chapter 15. I took this policy two years ago, in 2023, but looking back, I wish I'd done it sooner. I first learned about term insurance in 2011, when I was just starting to get serious about my finances. If I'd taken it back then, the premiums would've been much lower. But I missed that bus. It's not about regret—it's about realization and correcting the mistake. The wisest option is to get term or life insurance with your very first salary. It's as logical as that. The sooner you start, the better, because premiums are locked in for the entire tenure, and they're cheaper when you're younger.

***

One last thing—and this is crucial—don't confuse insurance with investment. I can't stress this enough. Insurance is not meant to grow your money; it's meant to protect what you've already built—your time, your effort, your resources, and your future. I've seen too many people fall into the trap of buying insurance policies that promise "returns" while charging high premiums and delivering poor value. Stay away from anyone who tells you insurance is an investment. It's a shield, not a sword. Use it to safeguard, not to chase gains. I know this mistake firsthand. I didn't fall for it once—I fell for it four times. And financially, those were some of the biggest missteps I've made. Together, they cost me the equivalent of 2.5 years' worth of monthly expenses. These policies didn't beat inflation—but they did offer periodic payouts: annually, every four years, and eventually after ten years. Realizing the mistake late wasn't the problem; I simply wasn't financially literate when I made them. What matters is that I learned and corrected course. Today, while those policies still don't keep up with inflation, they've been reassigned a different purpose in my financial plan.

They're no longer my growth engines—they're just slow-moving parts of a broader, more intentional strategy.

This chapter ties back to everything I've been saying since the beginning of this book. Preparing for the worst isn't about living in fear—it's about living with intention. It's about obeying yourself, so you're not commanded by life's uncertainties. It's about facing reality, so inflation or emergencies don't erode what you've earned. From health insurance to emergency funds, from home insurance to term insurance, these are the shields that let me sleep tight at night. I've spent 18 years learning from my early mistakes in 2007 to the disciplined choices of 2024.

Envision the worst, take the best options possible, and rest easy knowing you're prepared.

***

Chapter 17: Deposits and Banks: Securing What's Yours

The hard-earned money you've fought for is only truly yours as long as it's secure. That's a truth I've learned over my journey. Securing your money isn't just a task—it's one of the toughest battles you'll face. Money, at its core, is an instrument we need daily to keep life moving forward. But as Aristotle wisely said, "Money... exists not by nature, but by law." We're no longer animals surviving in the wild, where strength or instinct determines our fate. In today's world, money is what distinguishes individual capacity, what sets us apart. When money speaks, we need to make it count. But here's the catch: its value is entirely in the hands of the government. They could wake up tomorrow and declare paper money is no longer legal tender. It's possible—history has seen it happen, like India's demonetization in 2016, which I witnessed indirectly from the US. Money only holds value as long as the government says it does. Until that changes, it's our responsibility to protect it.

One of the safest ways to secure your money is by booking a deposit in a bank. In the post-COVID era inflation has become a hot topic, as I discussed in Chapter 15. Quantitative easing, the government's tactic of printing money to keep the nation running, has driven inflation higher, but it's also pushed interest rates up. Today, booking a deposit in a large private bank or a government bank is a safer bet than ever. These institutions offer stability, especially in uncertain times. For the best yields,

I recommend opting for a longer duration—typically 13 months—which often gives the highest returns. Right now, rates are hovering around 7.5% per annum, a decent deal considering the economic climate.

***

This is exactly where I park my emergency funds, which I talked about in Chapter 16. My emergency fund sits in a fixed deposit at 7.5% per annum, giving me both yield and security. It's a practical choice for funds you might need but not immediately, like emergencies or planned expenses. But there's a catch: in India, the interest from these deposits is taxable. That's a point you can't afford to overlook when planning your finances. If you're not accounting for taxes, you're not seeing the full picture of your returns.

To manage this, I've found a strategy that works for me: open multiple deposits instead of one. Each deposit has the same tenure—13 months in my case—but I choose different payout options for the interest. For example, one deposit might pay out monthly, another quarterly, a third half-yearly, and one annually. This way, I'm spreading the interest income throughout the year, which helps mitigate the tax burden by keeping my taxable income more consistent. Plus, I take that interest and reinvest it into direct stocks or mutual funds, aiming for higher growth. By doing this, I'm growing my money in two places at once, in different quantities though: the fixed deposit provides a steady, safe return, while the stock market offers a chance at higher gains—often 12% or more, as I've aimed for since beating inflation became my focus in Chapter 15. The taxed amount from the deposit interest can often be offset by stock price rises, and the frequent inflows from interest payouts help with high-value expenses, like paying school fees or funding a family trip. There's a small downside: opting for frequent payouts usually means a slightly lower interest rate—maybe 0.25% less than a yearly payout—but I think it's worth it. This strategy has served me well, and while I remain open to new insights, it balances security with growth effectively.

***

But what about smaller banks? They often offer higher interest rates—around 9.5%, a full 2% more than the 7.5% you'd get from corporate or government banks. That extra 2% can make a big difference. For example, on a deposit of 1 million rupees, a 7.5% rate gives you 75,000 rupees annually, while 9.5% gives you 95,000 rupees—a difference of 20,000 rupees per year. That's not pocket change; over a few years, it adds up significantly. Considering these smaller banks isn't a bad option at all, especially if you're looking to maximize returns on money you can afford to lock away. But strategy is key here, and there's a bigger picture to consider.

Is it wise to park a lump sum in a single bank, whether it's a large or small one? Definitely not. To understand why, we need to look at how the banking system works in India. The Reserve Bank of India provides a default insurance of 500,000 rupees per account holder through the Deposit Insurance and Credit Guarantee Corporation (DICGC). But here's the fine print: if you have multiple accounts in the same bank, that 500,000-rupee insurance applies only once per person, not per account. In other words, no matter how many accounts you have in one bank, you're only insured for up to 500,000 rupees total. This is the central bank's guarantee, meant to protect depositors if a bank fails. Knowing this, it's wise to spread your money across different banks, ensuring no single bank holds more than 500,000 rupees of your funds. That way, even if a bank goes bankrupt, your money is safe up to that limit in each institution.

This is where vigilance comes in, and it's a lesson I've taken to heart. Nietzsche once said, "Trusting the State's vaults is the comfort of the herd, a surrender of individual strength to the abstract promise of collective security." I couldn't agree more. We can't just blindly trust banks—big or small—based on their reputation. The world is unpredictable. A massive scam could surface at any time, or a bank could collapse under economic pressure. I've seen enough uncertainty in my career, from the 2016 demonetization in India to the global economic shocks post-COVID, to know that nothing is guaranteed. Have I already spread my money across multiple banks? Not yet. My current deposits are still locked in their 13-month tenures, but I've been contemplating this strategy and plan to act once they mature. For now, I'm keeping a close eye on my accounts, ensuring I'm not overexposed in any single bank.

***

Protecting your money comes down to having a strategy and sticking to it—unless it's proven wrong. All we can do is act on our best judgment, reflect, and correct course if needed. That's been my approach since the beginning of this journey, from my early mistakes with insurance policies in Chapter 16 to my disciplined saving habits in Chapter 14. Whether it's choosing the right bank, diversifying deposits, or reinvesting interest, the goal is the same: secure what's yours while making it work for you. In a world where money's value is a legal fiction, as Aristotle reminded us, it's up to us to ensure it doesn't slip through our fingers.

***

Chapter 18: Investments: Growing What You've Secured

We live in a world brimming with opportunities—opportunities that have the power to create wealth. And once that wealth is in your hands, it's not enough to simply hold onto it; it must be preserved and grown. That's where investment comes in—the act of allocating money to an asset class with the expectation of increasing your capital over time. The future can be short-term or long-term, depending on your goals. For instance, if you invest 100 rupees today, you might reasonably expect it to grow to 150 in the next two to three years—That's roughly 14–15% annually—just enough to be worthwhile. But not all options deliver the same results. Some promise higher returns, others offer stability, and a few prioritize safety. The key is understanding what fits your life, your risk tolerance, and your vision for the future.

We toil hard to earn our money, pouring in time, effort, and sweat. Leaving it idle feels like a missed opportunity—it should work for you even while you sleep. There's a certain pleasure in that, in watching your money generate more money on its own. As Seneca wisely said, "Wealth is the slave of a wise man." When we approach investing with intention, we refine our choices and make them work perfectly. Relying solely on earnings to build wealth would take three or four lifetimes to achieve what we dream of. Instead, investing in the right places can do the heavy lifting for us, turning our hard work into a legacy that grows beyond our active hours.

***

For me, stocks have been one of the better options to make this happen. There are countless ways to dive into the stock market—buying individual stocks, investing in mutual funds that bundle a basket of stocks, focusing on thematic investments, or even exploring unlisted stocks. My journey with stocks began early in my career, back when I was part of a startup in the late 2000s. What I did back then, I'd call more profit booking than investing. I'd buy a stock based on a colleague's tip and sell it the same day, the next day, or within a week as soon as I saw a profit. I did this for about a year, treating it like a quick game. Then life got busy, and I forgot about it, leaving some stocks dormant in my portfolio—untouched relics of my early experimentation.

As my career evolved, I shifted gears. Around 2009, I turned to fixed deposits, which were offering close to 9% returns at the time. This was a game-changer for me. I set up an account where any excess money would automatically move into a deposit account if I didn't use it—out of sight, out of reach, with no debit card to tempt me. That strategy funded significant moments in my life: my thread ceremony, parts of my sister's marriage expenses, and I still hold a few of those accounts from way back. It was a safe, steady way to grow money while keeping it secure, aligning with the lessons from Chapter 17 about protecting what's yours.

***

When I moved to the US, my approach to investing took a different turn. For nearly three years, I parked all my money in a savings account—safe, but not growing much. It wasn't until later that I re-entered the stock market, this time with a broader perspective. I also dipped my toes into cryptocurrencies, intrigued by their potential. One tool that revolutionized my investing was an app that tracked my credit and debit card transactions, rounding up purchases to invest the change. For example, if I spent $3.30, it would invest the $0.70 difference into the stock market. This automatic investing became a habit, building wealth incrementally without much effort. While a direct "round-up" investment app might not be universally available or as seamlessly integrated with Indian banking systems yet, the core principle—automating small, consistent investments from your spending—is incredibly powerful and universally applicable. Think of it this way: for every 100 rupees you spend, commit to saving or investing 10 rupees. This 10% rule isn't fixed; it's a flexible guideline. You could aim for 5 rupees for every 100, or even 20, depending on your income and lifestyle. The key is to make it a habitual, non-negotiable deduction from your spending.

Alongside this, my 401(k) savings plan was a lifeline, and the Employee Stock Ownership Plan (ESOP) I opted into during my last year in the US yielded solid returns. But it was during the COVID-19 pandemic, with its economic uncertainty, that my mindset shifted. Thoughts of the worst crept in—job loss, market crashes—and I began preparing seriously. My spouse and I turned to YouTube, diving into stock market tutorials, especially trading based on technical patterns. We dreamed of trading from the US into the Indian market, but that plan never took off due to regulatory hurdles.

***

Returning to India in 2021, we decided to give trading a proper shot. We opened separate accounts—my spouse for trading, me for investing. Trading, we soon learned, was a gamble, relying on same-day buys and sells driven by technical charts. After a few setbacks, we realized it wasn't for us, and thankfully, we figured this out early before losing a fortune. Our losses were minimal, but the pattern was clear: we'd correct one mistake only to make another. With hundreds of potential errors still ahead, we said goodbye to trading. Since then, we've stuck to investing, erasing trading from our minds. Now, we invest in stocks monthly—I focus on individual stocks with similar amounts in mutual funds. Spreading risk is crucial—who wants to expose everything to a single failure? My portfolio balances growth and stability through US stocks, Indian stocks, gold—and at one point, crypto. I choose avenues where I see returns while keeping safer options in the mix.

***

When picking investments, I look for companies that could survive even a nuclear attack—think Coca-Cola. For decades, Coke has weathered wars, recessions, and shifts in taste. It's not merely its longevity, but its globally ubiquitous brand, essential-like product, vast distribution network, and consistent demand that makes it remarkably resilient across diverse economic cycles. Will it disappear in the next few years? I can't guarantee it, but I see no reason it should. Build an investment thesis—why you're buying, what you expect—and stick to it, revising as market conditions change. Stocks, gold, and crypto aren't the only options. Real estate, government bonds, and investing in yourself (e.g., learning a new skill to double your salary) are worth considering. I focus on stocks and self-improvement because that's my strength, but I'm not a fan of real estate investing. The initial investment is high, and the yields don't match—rental income or appreciation rarely justifies it. If you buy with a loan, the repayment burden haunts you, eroding peace of mind. I'd argue it's not worth it. And don't mistake buying a car for an investment—it's a depreciating asset. Drive it out of the showroom, and its value drops by 10% instantly. That's not investment—that's erosion in motion. That's a hard reality to accept.

Another key to investing is rotating capital. Have a thesis and stick to it. If you buy a stock aiming for a 15% return, sell it once you hit that profit and reinvest in the next opportunity. No sentimentality— greed is the surest way to lose the golden egg. If you miss further gains after selling, so be it; the market will offer new chances. Limit any single stock to 5% of your total portfolio—say, no more than 20-25 stocks—to manage risk. If no opportunities arise after profit booking, shift to gold, US stocks, or crypto, but evaluate carefully. Rotate capital to realize real profits, because unrealized gains are promises, not progress.

Finally, a fourth-grader's wisdom still holds true: buy cheap, sell dear. It sounds simple, but timing is everything—wait for the right moment to buy low. Buy the dips. If a stock drops from □100 to □80, that's a 20% loss. But to climb back from □80 to □100, it needs to rise 25%. The numbers may seem similar, but the effort isn't symmetrical—losses cut deeper than gains heal. As Warren Buffett famously said, "The stock market is a device for transferring money from the impatient to the patient." Patience and discipline are your greatest allies.

***

Be an opportunist: dive boldly into spaces where you see potential, but don't freeze in hesitation—hesitation is the enemy of momentum. Go deep, play smart, and make your money work as hard as you do. Investing is about control—of your capital and your choices—and about self-awareness: knowing your past mistakes, like my early trading blunders, and learning from them.

This is your journey, your wealth, your future. Invest with clarity, conviction, and care—and let it shape the life you've always wanted to write. In the end, investing is more than a financial move. It's a declaration—not just of belief in the market, but of belief in yourself.

***

Chapter 19: SIP/SWP: Habits of Wealth and Control

Investment isn't a one-time leap—it's a long, steady process that fuels our progress. As your income flows in month after month, your investments should grow in tandem. But to make that happen, you need the right mindset, a deliberate choice to prioritize growth over stagnation. Just as we manage fixed and variable expenses each month, we must carve out fixed or incremental investments. This isn't just about safeguarding wealth; it's about cultivating a habit that shapes your financial destiny. As Aristotle rightly said, "We are what we repeatedly do. Excellence, then, is not an act, but a habit." Your deeds define you, and in our financial journey, our discipline and respect for money dictate who we are and who we become. It's no different from a career—if we lack progressive habits, we stagnate. The same holds true for money matters: habits are the bedrock of success.

Habits play a pivotal role here. If you're habituated to discretionary spending—impulse buys, unnecessary luxuries—you're letting money slip through your fingers. But if you're habituated to saving and investing, you're thinking ahead, letting your money grow. Reflecting on my own path, this lesson took root early. Right from my days at an Indian MNC in the late 2000s, I made it a habit to save more than 50% of my salary, funneling it into an unused bank account that automatically opened a deposit account. That wasn't a one-off decision; it was a habit I deliberately built, one that carried me throughout my career. It's a practice that echoes Chapter 17's focus on securing what's yours, proving that consistency can turn small actions into significant outcomes.

***

Systematic Investment Plans (SIPs) are a powerful way to ingrain this habit. They encourage you to set aside a fixed amount each month by a certain date, which is then invested into mutual funds. But SIPs aren't limited to mutual funds anymore—today, you can use them for direct stocks too. Don't confine the concept to just these options, though. What I did with my deposit accounts—automatically moving excess money into a growth vehicle—is another variant of SIP, tailored to a different instrument. The core problem SIPs solve is habituation: training yourself to save and invest regularly, turning intention into action. This aligns with Aristotle's wisdom—excellence through repetition.

SIPs, especially in mutual funds, are ideal for those who lack the time or expertise to pick individual stocks. There's nothing wrong with that—it's a practical choice. I lean toward index funds for this purpose, though I've invested in few other market themes across various mutual funds. Direct mutual funds appeal to me because they offer lower expense ratios and exit loads, often 0% on exit, minimizing costs. These funds are safe bets because stock indices are designed to grow over time. All-time highs aren't one-off events; they happen regularly, signaling that market money is expanding. Sure, events like COVID-19 or random geopolitical conflicts can shake things up, but unless you need to liquidate during those dips, they shouldn't derail you. In fact, I see those downturns as opportunities. Rather than relying solely on automated SIPs, I make it a habit to invest myself every month. I would do a lump sum in funds that underperformed the previous month. This downward averaging keeps capital flowing and balances my portfolio. Choose your asset class—stocks, mutual funds, or even deposits—and start investing. Make it a habit, and it will reward you in the long run. One day, you'll thank that disciplined version of yourself.

***

But growing wealth is only one side of the coin. The other—just as vital—is knowing how to draw from it wisely. Systematic Withdrawal Plans (SWPs) offer a way to withdraw money periodically over a predetermined period, keeping the power of your finances in your hands. This concept hit home for me when I bought my house loan-free with the savings from my US tenure, a personal triumph I detailed earlier. Looking back, I made a mistake by not utilizing SWP—I didn't even know it existed then, so I can't fault myself too harshly. With SWP, you deposit a lump sum into a fund, choose a withdrawal amount, and let it deposit that sum into your bank account monthly while the rest remains invested. The invested portion grows with market movements, giving you both a steady income and continued growth. It's a dual benefit that eluded me back then.

Imagine if I'd used SWP for that house purchase. I could have deposited my savings into a fund, taken a 15–20-year mortgage, and used SWP withdrawals to cover the EMIs. The difference would have been transformative. I wouldn't have faced the stress of a decades-long repayment, and after 20 years, I'd still have a significant corpus left in the fund, even after clearing the mortgage. As Seneca rightly pointed out, "Most powerful is he who has himself in his own power." SWP embodies this control, letting you dictate your financial needs and actions. It was a missed opportunity for me, but a valuable lesson. Have you been in a similar spot? If so, it's a learning moment for you too. If not, recognizing this now could save you from a future regret.

This philosophy ties back to my stance from Chapter 13—don't buy anything unless you can afford it in full. Pair that with SWP, and you gain peace of mind, a rarity in today's fast-paced world. Take buying a car, for instance. If I were to get one, I'd definitely use SWP. Deposit a lump sum, withdraw monthly to cover payments, and let the remaining corpus grow. It's a win-win: you enjoy the car while your investment continues to appreciate. Remember, growth depends on market movements, but it's reasonable to assume markets are designed to rise over time, a principle I've seen play out since my early investing days in Chapter 18.

Beyond just peace of mind, SWPs offer immense practical value. They can be set up to withdraw monthly, quarterly, or even annually, adapting to your lifestyle needs. They're particularly powerful in retirement, providing a steady, customizable income stream without depleting your entire corpus at once. This flexibility makes SWP ideal for anyone transitioning into financial independence or navigating post-retirement life. It's like having your cake, eating it slowly, and still watching it grow.

***

At the end of the day, SIPs and SWPs are methodologies to cultivate the habit of investing and maintain control over your finances. SIPs build the discipline to save and grow wealth, turning intention into a routine that compounds over years—much like my 50% savings habit from the MNC days. SWPs give you the reins to withdraw strategically, ensuring your money serves your life's milestones without sacrificing future growth. Together, they reflect the self-authorship I've championed throughout this book. From securing money in Chapter 17 to growing it in Chapter 18, these tools let you write your financial fate with intention.

This approach resonates as I've learned that wealth isn't just about numbers—it's about the habits and control that shape who you become. Start small, stay consistent, and let these systems work for you. Your future self will thank you for the legacy you're building today.

***

Chapter 20: Growth, Passive Income, and Taxes: Balancing Progress and Preservation

We all work hard to earn a living—it's become a daily rhythm, a grind that defines much of our existence. To secure our future, the thumb rule is clear: save and invest. But to secure our present, we must invest in ourselves and spend on our needs—a universally understandable cycle we're all looped into. This duality of growth and sustenance drives our financial journey. We venture into various asset classes with high hopes, expecting the best from our investments. Yet, we must never grow complacent. Once your hard-earned money moves from your bank account to an investment, it becomes your responsibility to track its performance. Assets will generally rise over the long term, but that ascent isn't a straight line—there are dips and downturns along the way. Still, significant dips rarely reduce a diversified portfolio to zero; a recovery always follows. As an investor, though, checking your portfolio daily is a futile exercise. Investments are for the long haul, not for daily obsessions.

As Spinoza wisely noted, "The mind, guided by reason, understands that the diligent augmentation of one's resources is a necessary act of self-preservation." This rationality, not sentiment, should guide us as we preserve and grow our wealth. I've learned this through experience. I track my portfolio once a month, jotting down notes to assess its health. This doesn't mean leaving it untouched—far from it. A good portfolio, in my view, might have 30% of its stocks underperforming, like weeds that need pruning. These laggards not only drag down overall returns but also lock capital in unproductive assets. The best approach is to sell them off, freeing that capital for rotation into stronger performers. Sometimes, though, downward averaging—buying more of an underperforming stock to lower its average cost—makes sense, depending on market dynamics and the sector. For instance, during a sector-wide dip in technology stocks in 2022, I chose to average down on a promising firm rather than sell, and it paid off when the sector rebounded.

***

Selling underperforming assets serves a dual purpose: it removes blockages and enables tax harvesting. Tax harvesting is the strategy of offsetting gains with losses to delay or reduce tax liability. Imagine you book a profit of 100,000 rupees in a financial year with no losses—your taxes align with your slab rate, potentially eating into a significant chunk. But if you sell a few underperforming stocks at a loss, say 20,000 rupees, your net profit drops to 80,000 rupees, lowering your tax burden. Ayn Rand's words ring true here: "Taxation, when it exceeds the bare protection of individual rights, it is the sacrifice of the productive to the unproductive, a moral bankruptcy disguised as civic duty." Understanding tax rates is crucial—taxes, like inflation from Chapter 15, are another thief of wealth. Working around them is a wise choice.

Similarly, when you buy stocks in the US market, you are only taxed once. If you have paid US taxes, there is no need to pay Indian taxes though you may still need to declare these earnings in India and claim foreign tax credits as per DTAA guidelines. This double taxation avoidance stems from the India-US tax treaty, a benefit I leveraged when investing in US equities. Gold bonds are tax-free in India. They offer yearly interest and also the real price appreciation at the end of the tenure—another good option to consider. I explored these bonds in 2021 after returning to India, drawn by their stability and tax advantage, especially when reinvesting deposit income from Chapter 17. These options diversify your portfolio while minimizing tax drag, aligning with the rational self-preservation Spinoza advocated.

A key aspect is distinguishing between short-term and long-term capital gains tax. In India, short-term gains (assets held less than a year) might be taxed at 20%, while long-term gains (over a year) could be 10%. If you're considering selling an underperforming asset in the 11th month, is it worth it? It depends on the capital tied up and the re-investment opportunity. Waiting another month to qualify for the lower long-term rate could save you 10%—a decision I weighed carefully when trimming my portfolio in 2023. This rational approach, guided by Spinoza's self-preservation, ensures your money works harder for you.

***

Alongside growth and tax management, a constant flow of passive income is essential. Remember the fixed deposits from Chapter 17? They provided a steady passive income—monthly, quarterly, semi-annually, and annually— which I reinvested into other asset classes for further growth. This income has been enough to cover annual school fees and term insurance premiums, etc., freeing my regular earnings for other priorities. Passive income acts as a cushion, giving you confidence to pursue bigger goals.

I've also learned from mistakes. One significant misstep was an endowment plan I bought years ago with a lump sum. It promised a fixed yearly income from year two until I turn 100, paired with term insurance for the same amount. While it was a poor investment choice—lacking the growth of stocks or mutual funds—the yearly payout now funds a better endowment plan for my spouse. It's not ideal, but something is better than nothing. Surrendering it would incur high losses, so I've turned it into a win-win: the income offsets the mistake while providing a regular stream. This adaptability reflects the control I've sought since Chapter 13's rejection of unnecessary debt.

Other passive income sources I've explored include dividends from stocks I've held. These streams, though modest, reinforce the idea that passive income isn't just about luxury— it's a foundation of financial resilience. Reinvesting these earnings into index funds or gold, as I did during the 2021 market recovery, compounds their value, aligning with Chapter 19's habit-building ethos.

***

All these components—portfolio maintenance, tax planning, and passive income—must come together like gears in a well-oiled machine. Ultimately, growing money, securing passive income, and protecting it from taxes are interconnected goals. Tracking your portfolio monthly, pruning underperformers, and harvesting tax losses keep your capital dynamic, as I've done since so many years. Passive income cushions your present, letting you invest in yourself—whether through skills (doubling my salary with a new certification in 2019) or experiences—while tax strategies preserve your gains. The approach that I've learned that true wealth lies in this balance—growth fueled by habit, income for security, and taxes managed with foresight. Act now, and shape the future you're destined to write.

***

A Heartfelt Farewell, Dear Reader

As we arrive at the final chapter of this shared journey, I pause to reflect on the incredible path we've walked together through these pages. This book is a tapestry of stories, ideas, and emotions—and your presence as a reader has added its most vibrant threads.

I hope these words have brought you moments of joy, quiet contemplation, and perhaps even a spark of inspiration to carry into your own life. Writing this has been a labor of passion and discovery, and knowing you've been alongside me has made it all the more rewarding.

As you close this book, I invite you to let its lessons and dreams settle into your heart, guiding you forward into whatever comes next. Whether we meet again in the pages of another work or in the silent spaces where imagination thrives, I wish you clarity, strength, and happiness.

If there's one lesson, I leave you with, let it be this: the habits we choose, and the control we take, shape everything we become.

Thank you for being part of this experience—your presence has made it unforgettable.

Bharani Vir Bhatla

In gratitude to the philosophers who taught me to see the meaning behind the coin and the power behind the pen.